AAT

Qualifications and Credit Framework (QCF)

AQ2013

LEVEL 4 DIPLOMA IN ACCOUNTING

TEXT

Option Paper:
Business Tax
FA 2014

2014 Edition

For assessments from January 2015

Second edition August 2014
ISBN 9781 4727 0909 7

Previous edition
ISBN 9781 4727 0322 4

British Library Cataloguing-in-Publication Data
A catalogue record for this book is available from the British
Library

Published by
BPP Learning Media Ltd
BPP House
Aldine Place
London
W12 8AA

www.bpp.com/learningmedia

Printed in the United Kingdom by Martins of Berwick

Martins of Berwick
Sea View Works
Spittal
Berwick-Upon-Tweed
TD15 1RS

Your learning materials, published by BPP Learning Media Ltd,
are printed on paper sourced from traceable sustainable sources.

CONTENTS

BPP LEARNING MEDIA'S AAT MATERIALS

The AAT's assessments fall within the **Qualifications and Credit Framework** and most papers are assessed by way of an on demand **computer based assessment**. BPP Learning Media has invested heavily to ensure our materials are as relevant as possible for this method of assessment. In particular, our **suite of online resources** ensures that you are prepared for online testing by allowing you to practise numerous online tasks that are similar to the tasks you will encounter in the AAT's assessments.

Resources

The BPP range of resources comprises:

- **Texts**, covering all the knowledge and understanding needed by students, with numerous illustrations of 'how it works', practical examples and tasks for you to use to consolidate your learning. The majority of tasks within the texts have been written in an interactive style that reflects the style of the online tasks we anticipate the AAT will set. When you purchase a Text you are also granted free access to your Text content online.

- **Question Banks**, including additional learning questions plus the AAT's sample assessment(s) and a number of BPP full practice assessments. Full answers to all questions and assessments, prepared by BPP Learning Media Ltd, are included. Our question banks are provided free of charge in an online environment containing tasks similar to those you will encounter in the AAT's testing environment. This means you can become familiar with being tested in an online environment prior to completing the real assessment.

- **Passcards**, which are handy pocket-sized revision tools designed to fit in a handbag or briefcase to enable you to revise anywhere at anytime. All major points are covered in the Passcards which have been designed to assist you in consolidating knowledge.

- **Workbooks**, which have been designed to cover the units that are assessed by way of computer based project/case study. The workbooks contain many practical tasks to assist in the learning process and also a sample assessment or project to work through.

- **Lecturers' resources**, for units assessed by computer based assessments. These provide a further bank of tasks, answers and full practice assessments for classroom use, available separately only to lecturers whose colleges adopt BPP Learning Media material.

This Text for Business Tax has been written specifically to ensure comprehensive yet concise coverage for the AAT's **AQ2013** learning outcomes and assessment criteria.

Each chapter contains:

- Clear, step by step explanation of the topic

- Logical progression and linking from one chapter to the next

- Numerous illustrations of 'how it works'

- Interactive tasks within the text of the chapter itself, with answers at the back of the book. The majority of these tasks have been written in the interactive form that students can expect to see in their real assessments

- Test your learning questions of varying complexity, again with answers supplied at the back of the book. The majority of these questions have been written in the interactive form that students can expect to see in their real assessments

The emphasis in all tasks and test questions is on the practical application of the skills acquired.

Supplements

From time to time we may need to publish supplementary materials to one of our titles. This can be for a variety of reasons, from a small change in the AAT unit guidance to new legislation coming into effect between editions.

You should check our supplements page regularly for anything that may affect your learning materials. All supplements are available free of charge on our supplements page on our website at:

http://www.bpp.com/about-bpp/aboutBPP/StudentInfo#q4

Customer feedback

If you have any comments about this book, please email ianblackmore@bpp.com or write to Ian Blackmore, AAT Range Manager, BPP Learning Media Ltd, BPP House, Aldine Place, London W12 8AA.

Any feedback we receive is taken into consideration when we periodically update our materials, including comments on style, depth and coverage of AAT standards.

In addition, although our products pass through strict technical checking and quality control processes, unfortunately errors may occasionally slip through when producing material to tight deadlines.

When we learn of an error in a batch of our printed materials, either from internal review processes or from customers using our materials, we want to make sure customers are made aware of this as soon as possible and the appropriate action is taken to minimise the impact on student learning.

As a result, when we become aware of any such errors we will:

1) Include details of the error and, if necessary, PDF prints of any revised pages under the related subject heading on our 'supplements' page at: http://www.bpp.com/about-bpp/aboutBPP/StudentInfo#q4

2) Update the source files ahead of any further printing of the materials.

3) Investigate the reason for the error and take appropriate action to minimise the risk of reoccurrence.

A NOTE ON TERMINOLOGY

The AAT AQ2013 standards and assessments use international terminology based on International Financial Reporting Standards (IFRSs). Although you may be familiar with UK terminology, you need to now know the equivalent international terminology for your assessments.

The following information is taken from an article on the AAT's website and compares IFRS terminology with UK GAAP terminology. It then goes on to describe the impact of IFRS terminology on students studying for each level of the AAT QCF qualification.

Note that since the article containing the information below was published, there have been changes made to some IFRSs. Therefore BPP Learning Media have updated the table and other information below to reflect these changes.

In particular, the primary performance statement under IFRSs which was formerly known as the 'income statement' or the 'statement of comprehensive income' is now called the 'statement of profit or loss' or the 'statement of profit or loss and other comprehensive income'.

What is the impact of IFRS terms on AAT assessments?

The list shown in the table that follows gives the 'translation' between UK GAAP and IFRS.

UK GAAP	IFRS
Final accounts	Financial statements
Trading and profit and loss account	**Statement of profit or loss (or statement of profit or loss and other comprehensive income)**
Turnover or Sales	Revenue or Sales Revenue
Sundry income	Other operating income
Interest payable	Finance costs
Sundry expenses	Other operating costs
Operating profit	Profit from operations
Net profit/loss	Profit/Loss for the year/period
Balance sheet	**Statement of financial position**
Fixed assets	Non-current assets
Net book value	Carrying amount
Tangible assets	Property, plant and equipment

UK GAAP	IFRS
Reducing balance depreciation	Diminishing balance depreciation
Depreciation/Depreciation expense(s)	Depreciation charge(s)
Stocks	Inventories
Trade debtors or Debtors	Trade receivables
Prepayments	Other receivables
Debtors and prepayments	Trade and other receivables
Cash at bank and in hand	Cash and cash equivalents
Trade creditors or Creditors	Trade payables
Accruals	Other payables
Creditors and accruals	Trade and other payables
Long-term liabilities	Non-current liabilities
Capital and reserves	Equity (limited companies)
Profit and loss balance	Retained earnings
Minority interest	Non-controlling interest
Cash flow statement	**Statement of cash flows**

This is certainly not a comprehensive list, which would run to several pages, but it does cover the main terms that you will come across in your studies and assessments. However, you won't need to know all of these in the early stages of your studies – some of the terms will not be used until you reach Level 4. For each level of the AAT qualification, the points to bear in mind are as follows:

Level 2 Certificate in Accounting

The IFRS terms do not impact greatly at this level. Make sure you are familiar with 'receivables' (also referred to as 'trade receivables'), 'payables' (also referred to as 'trade payables'), and 'inventories'. The terms sales ledger and purchases ledger – together with their control accounts – will continue to be used. Sometimes the control accounts might be called 'trade receivables control account' and 'trade payables control account'. The other term to be aware of is 'non-current asset' – this may be used in some assessments.

Level 3 Diploma in Accounting

At this level you need to be familiar with the term 'financial statements'. The financial statements comprise a 'statement of profit or loss' (previously known as an income statement), and a 'statement of financial position'. In the statement of profit or loss the term 'revenue' or 'sales revenue' takes the place of 'sales', and 'profit for the year' replaces 'net profit'. Other terms may be used in the statement of financial position – eg 'non-current assets' and 'carrying amount'. However, specialist limited company terms are not required at this level.

Level 4 Diploma in Accounting

At Level 4 a wider range of IFRS terms is needed, and in the case of Financial statements, are already in use – particularly those relating to limited companies. Note especially that a statement of profit or loss becomes a 'statement of profit or loss and other comprehensive income'.

Note: The information above was taken from an AAT article from the 'assessment news' area of the AAT website (www.aat.org.uk). However, it has been adapted by BPP Learning Media for changes in international terminology since the article was published and for any changes needed to reflect the move from AQ2010 to AQ2013.

ASSESSMENT STRATEGY

This unit will be assessed via a computer based test of two hour duration. The competency level is set at 70 per cent.

To be successful, learners should demonstrate robust knowledge and understanding of the unit in all tax areas. Learners cannot avoid any of the key topics and to ensure success, must be prepared to answer written and computational style questions in any of the tasks.

For AQ2013 the Business Tax assessment consists of eleven tasks:

Task	Maximum marks	Title for topics within task range
1	12	Computation of adjusted profits for sole traders, partnerships and limited companies
2	14	Computation of capital allowances for sole traders, partnerships and limited companies
3	12	Split of partnership profits for new, continuing and leaving partners. Basis periods for sole traders and partnerships
4	12	Taxable total profits and corporation tax payable
5	4	National insurance contributions
6	6	Losses for sole traders, partnerships and limited companies
7	10	Theory underpinning topic, payments on account and penalties
8	6	Tax returns
9	8	Basics of capital gains tax
10	10	Taxation of shares
11	6	Capital gains tax exemptions, losses, reliefs and tax payable

QCF Level descriptor	Summary
	Achievement at level 4 reflects the ability to identify and use relevant understanding, methods and skills to address problems that are well defined but complex and non-routine. It includes taking responsibility for overall courses of action as well as exercising autonomy and judgement within fairly broad parameters. It also reflects understanding of different perspectives or approaches within an area of study or work. **Knowledge and understanding** ■ Practical, theoretical or technical understanding to address problems that are well defined but complex and non routine ■ Analyse, interpret and evaluate relevant information and ideas ■ Be aware of the nature and approximate scope of the area of study or work ■ Have an informed awareness of different perspectives or approaches within the area of study or work **Application and action** ■ Address problems that are complex and non routine while normally fairly well defined ■ Identify, adapt and use appropriate methods and skills ■ Initiate and use appropriate investigation to inform actions ■ Review the effectiveness and appropriateness of methods, actions and results **Autonomy and accountability** ■ Take responsibility for courses of action, including where relevant, responsibility for the work of others ■ Exercise autonomy and judgement within broad but generally well-defined parameters

AAT UNIT GUIDE (AQ2013)

Business Tax

Introduction

Business tax covers the key taxes payable by sole traders, partnerships and limited companies. This includes income tax, national insurance, capital gains tax and corporation tax. It is a Level 4 unit for which learners need no prior knowledge.

Purpose of the unit

The general purpose of this unit is to enable learners to understand the impact and significance of taxation on both unincorporated and incorporated businesses. By studying these taxes, learners can appreciate the tax implications of financial decisions made by such organisations.

Learning objectives

By studying this unit the learner will be able to:

- Understand the impact of legislation and legislative changes.

- Understand tax law and its implications for unincorporated businesses.

- Understand tax law and its implications for incorporated businesses.

- Understand how to treat capital assets.

- Prepare the relevant pages of a tax return for an unincorporated business and accurately produce the computations to support this.

- Correctly complete corporation tax returns with all supporting computations for incorporated businesses.

Guidance on delivery

Adjusted profits:

This is a vital area for all business types as it is the start to the tax computation. Learners can expect to receive information which has been prepared under accounting rules, and need to adjust or amend appropriately for taxation rules. Such information could be for sole traders, partnerships or limited companies.

Learners can expect questions on:

- The differences between capital and revenue expenses

- The impact of private usage on assets and expenses

- Differences between the computation of profits and losses for unincorporated and incorporated businesses

- Tax allowable and disallowable expenses

Learners will mainly be required to complete computational style questions for this topic area, but some written tasks can be expected.

Capital allowances:

Always a complex area, learners must ensure that they are fully conversant with this topic. Not only must learners know how to do the calculations for plant and machinery, they must be able to explain these rules to tax payers. Capital allowances as they apply to opening, continuing and closing businesses must also be understood.

Specifically included areas are:

- All allowances, such as annual investment allowance, first year allowance and writing down allowance
- Rules from previous tax years as they would affect an accounting period ended during the relevant tax year
- Capital allowances periods that straddle tax years
- Computations of balancing allowances and balancing charges
- Cessation of trade situations
- Treatment of short life assets
- Difference in capital allowance treatment for unincorporated and incorporated business

Excluded topics:

Periods which commence prior to 1 January 2013.

Partnerships and basis periods

In relation to partnerships, there will be a maximum of three partners in any one scenario. Changes to partnerships will be assessed for changes to the partnership agreement and changes to the actual partners themselves.

The topic of basis periods could be for sole traders and/or partnerships. Therefore, learners can expect to see questions where the partnership has a new partner and/or a retiring partner, leading to computations of both the partnership profits and the profits assessable to tax under the basis periods rules.

Learners can expect questions on:

- Commencement of trade for a sole trader
- Continuation of trade for a sole trader
- Cessation of trade for a sole trader
- Computation of, and impact of, overlap profits

- Computation of partnership profits where the profit sharing ratio has changed, including salaries and interest on capital

- Computation of partnership profits where the partners have changed

- Impact of basis periods when there are changes to partners

Whilst these tasks will be mainly of a computational nature, learners must be prepared to provide written information for clients.

Excluded topics:

Change of accounting date
Limited liability partnerships

Incorporated businesses:

As the computation of trading profits, capital allowances and capital gains will be assessed in other tasks, learners will not be expected to calculate these figures again when tackling a task which combines these figures. Instead, learners will need to be able to show understanding of how all sources of income for incorporated businesses are used to compute the taxable total profits.

From there, learners may need to be able to calculate the corporation tax payable.

Specifically, learners can expect questions on:

- Computation of taxable total profits from:

  - Trading income
  - Property income
  - Investment income
  - Capital gains

- Qualifying charitable donations

- Accounting periods less than, equal to, or longer than, twelve months

- Computation of corporation tax payable including:

  - 31 March straddle
  - Impact of associated companies
  - All corporation tax rates
  - Due dates of payment for small and large companies

These questions will mainly be of a computational nature.

National Insurance:

This is only in relation to self-employed persons. Therefore, only Class 2 and Class 4 will need to be understood.

Excluded topics:

Class 1 and 3 NIC

Losses

Losses for both unincorporated and incorporated businesses can be expected.

For unincorporated businesses, learners can expect questions on:

- Carry forward of losses
- Losses to be set against other income in the year of the loss and carry back to the previous year
- Losses to be set against capital gains

For incorporated businesses, learners can expect questions on:

- Losses set against current profits
- Losses set against profits from earlier years
- Losses carried forward
- Impact of losses on relief for qualifying charitable donations

Both theory based questions and computational style questions can be expected within this topic area.

Excluded topics:

Losses in the early years of trading
Terminal loss relief
Time limits for claiming loss relief
Section numbers from the Acts

Written advice to clients:

Badges of trade will feature so that learners can demonstrate understanding of how to decide if a trade is being carried on. Learners may need to be able to consider various situations and scenarios, and apply the rules under the badges of trade to determine how HMRC would consider the situation in the light of trading.

Other, theory based, areas that underpin the entire specific taxation topic will be assessable within this area.

Learners can expect questions on:

- Explain what taxation documentation individuals need to maintain and for how long

- Explain implications of not providing full, accurate and timely tax information to HMRC

- Explain how the various penalties and interest are applied by HMRC for:
    - Late payment of both income tax and corporation tax
    - Late filing of tax returns
    - Fling of incorrect tax returns
    - Failing to notify of chargeability

- Explain the self-assessment process, including payments on account

- Computation of payments on account amounts, covering a number of years

This topic area will be assessed via a free text written response from the learner. The questions will usually be client focussed so learners will be expected to address their answers in a manner appropriate to such an audience.

Excluded topics:

Complex computations such as daily interest

Tax returns:

There are three tax returns which are assessable:

- Self-employment
- Partnerships
- CT600 short version

These are expected to be completed with accuracy and in conjunction with the learner's own figures, if appropriate.

Capital gains tax:

Learners must appreciate who and what is taxable under this heading. The impact that relationships between connected persons have on disposal of capital assets needs to be understood.

Computations can be expected on:

- Chargeable assets being disposed of

- Enhancement expenditure

- Part disposals

- Chattels

- Share disposals, including matching rules, bonus issues and rights issues as they apply to both individuals and companies

- Reliefs applicable to individuals, including:
    - Entrepreneurs' relief
    - Rollover relief
    - Gift relief

- Capital gains tax payable by individuals

- Annual exempt amount for individuals

- Relief for capital losses

- Indexation allowance for companies

There are three questions that cover this large topic, one of which will only consider the gains and losses for shares. This question will be humanly marked.

Excluded topics:

Takeovers and reorganisations
Small part disposals of land
Small part disposals rules as applicable to rights issues
Reinvestment relief
Computation of the indexation factor – this will be provided, if appropriate

TAXATION DATA

Taxation tables for Business Tax – 2014/15

Note that 'TAXATION DATA 1' and 'TAXATION DATA 2' shown below will be available as pop up windows throughout your live assessment.

TAXATION DATA 1

Capital allowances	
Annual investment allowance	
From 1 January 2013	£250,000
From 1/6 April 2014	£500,000
Plant and machinery writing down allowance	18%
Motor cars	
CO_2 emissions up to 95g/km	100%
CO_2 emissions between 96g/km and 130g/km	18%
CO_2 emissions over 130g/km	8%
Energy efficient and water saving plant	
First year allowance	100%
Capital gains	
Annual exempt amount	£11,000
Standard rate	18%
Higher rate (applicable over £31,865)	28%
Entrepreneurs' relief rate	10%
Entrepreneurs' relief limit	£10,000,000
National insurance rates	
Class 2 contributions:	£2.75 per week
Small earnings exception	£5,885 p.a
Class 4 contributions:	
Main rate	9%
Additional rate	2%
Lower profits limit	£7,956
Upper profits limit	£41,865

TAXATION DATA 2

Corporation tax		
Financial year	**2014**	**2013**
Small profits rate	20%	20%
Marginal relief:		
Lower limit	£300,000	£300,000
Upper limit	£1,500,000	£1,500,000
Standard fraction	1/400	3/400
Main rate	21%	23%
Marginal relief formula: Fraction $\times$ (U-A) $\times$ N/A		

chapter 1:
THE TAX FRAMEWORK

chapter coverage 📖

In this opening chapter we consider the various methods by which a business can operate. The method of operation affects how the business is taxed. We then see that the tax law governing businesses is included in both Acts of Parliament and a body of law known as case law.

Finally, we briefly consider how to calculate an individual's income tax liability. You may need to be aware of this when dealing with business losses.

The topics that we shall cover are:

✍ Methods of operating a business

✍ Relevant legislation and guidance from HMRC

✍ Calculating an individual's income tax liability

METHODS OF OPERATING A BUSINESS

A person wishing to operate a business could do so:

(a) As a sole trader (ie a self employed individual)
(b) In partnership with other self employed individuals
(c) Through a limited company

Business taxes

Sole traders and partnerships are unincorporated businesses. This means that there is no legal separation between the individual(s) carrying on the business and the business itself.

As a result the individual(s) concerned must pay:

- INCOME TAX on any income arising from the business
- CAPITAL GAINS TAX on any gains arising on the disposal of business assets

As a general rule, income is a receipt that is expected to recur (such as business profits), whereas a gain arises on a one-off disposal of a capital asset for a profit (eg the profit on the sale of a factory used in the business).

Sole traders and partners must also pay **National Insurance Contributions** (NICs) on their business profits.

Companies are incorporated businesses. This means they are taxed as separate legal entities independently of their owners.

Companies must pay:

- CORPORATION TAX on their total profits

Total profits include income arising from all sources and gains arising on the disposal of any assets.

Payment and administration of tax

Both companies and individuals must submit regular tax returns and pay any tax due by the due date. The due dates for submitting returns and paying tax differ for individuals and companies and will be looked at in Chapters 10 and 11 of this Text.

RELEVANT LEGISLATION AND GUIDANCE FROM HMRC

Statute law

Most of the rules governing income tax, capital gains tax and corporation tax are laid down in STATUTE LAW, which consists of Acts of Parliament.

The existing Acts are amended each year (as a result of the Budget) in the annual Finance Act(s). This Text includes the provisions of the **Finance Act 2014**. This Act will be assessed from 1 January 2015.

Some tax Acts provide for the making of detailed regulations by STATUTORY INSTRUMENT (SI). A SI must be laid before Parliament and will usually become law automatically within a stated period unless any objections to it are raised.

HMRC guidance

To help taxpayers, **HM Revenue and Customs (HMRC)**, which administers tax in the UK, publish a wide range of guidance material on how they interpret the various Acts. Much of this information can be found on HMRC's website **www.hmrc.gov.uk.** However, none of HMRC's guidance material has the force of law. Although you may like to have a look at this website, you should find all you need for assessment purposes within this Text.

Case law

Sometimes there may be a disagreement between HMRC and a taxpayer about how the tax legislation should be interpreted. In this situation either the taxpayer or HMRC may take the case to court. Cases about tax law are heard by the Tax Tribunal in the first instance.

Cases decided by the courts provide guidance on how legislation should be interpreted, and collectively form a second source of tax law known as CASE LAW.

You will not be expected to quote the names of decided cases in your assessment but you may need to know the principle decided in a case. Where relevant this will be noted within this Text.

CALCULATING AN INDIVIDUAL'S INCOME TAX LIABILITY

We now briefly consider how to calculate an individual's income tax liability. This will enable you to see how the knowledge you learn within the following chapters (specifically in relation to unincorporated businesses) fits into the larger picture. It will also help you when dealing with business losses later in this Text. However, detailed income tax computations are not assessed in the Business Tax assessment. You will deal with income tax computations if you study for the Personal Tax assessment.

Tax year

Individuals must prepare personal tax computations for tax years. A tax year (or fiscal year or year of assessment) is the year that runs from 6 April in one year to 5 April in the next. For example, the **2014/15 tax year** runs from **6 April 2014 to 5 April 2015**.

Components of income

As well as trading income from his business, an individual trader may receive various other types of income, such as employment income, rental income, bank and building society interest, and/or dividends. These different types of income are referred to as 'components'.

These components may be classed as **non-savings income, savings income, or dividend income**.

Savings income is interest (eg from a bank or building society). Dividend income is dividends received from companies. Non-savings income is any other type of income eg trading income, employment income and property income.

Total income, net income and taxable income

Example of an income tax computation for 2014/15

	Non-savings income £	Savings income £	Dividend income £	Total £
Trade profits	22,750			
Employment income	15,200			
Property income	3,400			
Building society interest (gross)		9,550		
Dividends (gross)			7,000	
Total income	**41,350**	**9,550**	**7,000**	**57,900**
Less trade losses	(2,000)	–	–	
Net income	**39,350**	**9,550**	**7,000**	**55,900**
Less personal allowance	(10,000)	–	–	
Taxable income	**29,350**	**9,550**	**7,000**	**45,900**

Each tax year (6 April – 5 April) all of an individual's components of income for that year must be added together to arrive at TOTAL INCOME.

Some items, such as trading losses, are deducted from total income to compute NET INCOME. In many cases total income and net income will be the same because there are no deductions to be made from total income. We therefore just show the amount of net income.

Individuals are entitled to a **personal allowance** which is deducted from net income to arrive at TAXABLE INCOME. Note that individuals born before 6 April 1948 are entitled to a higher personal allowance. The personal allowance effectively represents an amount of income that an individual may receive tax free. Where an individual has net income in excess of £100,000 the personal allowance is reduced, so that individuals with net income in excess of £120,000 receive no personal allowance.

Task 1

An individual has the following gross income in 2014/15

	£
Trading income	16,000
Building society interest	6,000
Dividends	8,750

His personal allowance is £10,000. His taxable income is:

£ [ ]

Income tax liability

The income is taxed in the following order:

(a) Non-savings income
(b) Savings income
(c) Dividend income

Non-savings income is taxed in three bands. Non-savings income up to £31,865 is taxed at 20%. This is called the **basic rate band**. Non-savings income above £31,865 up to £150,000 is taxed at 40%. This is called the **higher rate band**. Non-savings income above £150,000 is taxed at 45%. This is called the **additional rate band**.

There is a savings income starting rate of 10% that applies on savings income up to £2,880. However, because non-savings income is taxed first, if the individual has non-savings income that exceeds the starting rate threshold of £2,880, the starting rate will not apply. Savings income that does not fall within the starting rate band but falls within the basic rate band is taxed at 20%. Savings income in the higher rate band is taxed at 40% and savings income in the additional rate band is taxed at 45%.

Lastly, dividend income is taxed. If dividend income falls within the basic rate band, it is taxed at 10%. If, however, the dividend income falls in the higher rate band it is taxed at 32.5% and if it falls in the additional rate band it is taxed at 37.5%.

HOW IT WORKS

Zoë has taxable income (after the deduction of the personal allowance) of £40,000. Of this £21,000 is non-savings income, £10,000 is interest and £9,000 is dividend income.

Zoë's income tax liability for 2014/15 is calculated as follows:

			£
Non savings income			
	£21,000	× 20%	4,200
Savings income			
	£10,000	× 20%	2,000
Dividend income			
	£865	× 10%	87
	£8,135	× 32.5%	2,644
	9,000		
Tax liability			8,931

Task 2

Mark has taxable income of £50,000 for 2014/15. All of his income is non-savings income.

Mark's income tax liability is:

£	

HOW IT WORKS

Andreas has taxable income of £8,000. Of this, £2,000 is non-savings income and £6,000 is savings income.

His income tax liability for 2014/15 is calculated as follows:

			£
Non savings income			
	£2,000	× 20%	400
Savings income			
	£880	× 10%	88
	£5,120	× 20%	1,024
	£6,000		
Tax liability			1,512

Task 3

Jo has taxable income of £40,000. Of this, £1,500 is non-savings income, £30,000 is savings income and £8,500 is dividend income.

Jo's income tax liability for 2014/15 is:

£	

HOW IT WORKS

Clive has taxable income of £190,000. Of this £140,000 is non-savings income, £30,000 is interest and £20,000 is dividend income.

Clive's income tax liability for 2014/15 is calculated as follows:

			£
Non savings income			
	£31,865	× 20%	6,373
	£108,135	× 40%	43,254
	£140,000		
Savings income			
	£10,000	× 40%	4,000
	£20,000	× 45%	9,000
	£30,000		
Dividend income			
	£20,000	× 37.5%	7,500
Tax liability			70,127

Task 4

Sharon has taxable income of £175,000 for 2014/15. Of this £120,000 is non-savings income and £55,000 is dividend income. Sharon's income tax liability is:

£	

Assessment focus

The content of this chapter is designed to give you a basic overview of areas of the UK tax system that you might encounter within your AAT studies and also to help you understand how the content of this Business Tax Text fits into the bigger picture of the overall UK tax system.

You should not expect to see a task in the business tax assessment that is based purely on the contents of this chapter.

A note about rounding

Generally within the live assessment all answers should be given to the nearest whole pound unless the instruction to that task specifically states otherwise.

An exception to this is when you calculate National Insurance Contributions (NIC) for which the AAT will usually request that your answer be shown in pounds and pence.

When rounding is needed for an answer to an example or task, this Text has used the mathematical rounding rule of 0.5 and above being rounded up and anything below 0.5 being rounded down.

The AAT have told us that the computer will compensate for rounding differences and will accept a variety of answer formats (eg nil, NIL, Nil, 0, Zero ZERO).

However, always read the instructions provided by the AAT at the start of your assessment very carefully, as guidance will be given on how to input your answers. If any specific rounding rules are to be used they will be included within the guidance.

CHAPTER OVERVIEW

- A business may be operated by a sole trader, partnership or company
- Individuals trading as sole traders or in partnerships pay income tax, capital gains tax and NICs
- Companies suffer corporation tax
- Companies and individuals must submit regular tax returns
- All of an individual's components of income for a tax year are added together to arrive at total income
- Trading losses are deducted from total income to arrive at net income
- A personal allowance is deducted from net income to arrive at taxable income
- Taxable income is taxed at one of six rates, depending on which rate band it falls into and the type of income it is

Keywords

Total income – is the total of an individual's components of income for a tax year, from all sources

Net income – is total income minus for example trading losses

Taxable income – is an individual's net income minus the personal allowance

TEST YOUR LEARNING

Test 1

A company pays income tax on its total profits.

Show whether this statement is True or False?

TICK ONE BOX

	✓
True	
False	

Test 2

Complete the following statement.

Each tax year all of an individual's components of income are added together, then a personal allowance is deducted to arrive at:

| ▼ | .

Picklist:

Total income
Net income
Taxable income

Test 3

Arun (aged 35) has the following gross income in 2014/15:

Non-savings income	£25,000
Savings income	£12,000
Dividend income	£10,000

Calculate Arun's income tax liability for 2014/15. Show your answer in whole pounds.

£	

chapter 2:
COMPUTING TRADING INCOME

---

chapter coverage 📖

We start this chapter by looking at the factors that HMRC consider when deciding whether a trade is being carried on. We then look at the detailed rules that determine how taxable trading profits are calculated.

Finally, we look at the self employment tax pages which you may be required to complete in your assessment.

The topics that we shall cover are:

- ✎ Badges of trade
- ✎ Adjustment of profits
- ✎ Capital and revenue expenditure
- ✎ Allowable and disallowable expenditure
- ✎ Self employment tax return page

INTRODUCTION

Chapter 1 outlined different methods of operating a business. We saw that if a business is being operated as a sole trader or partnership, **income tax** will be paid on the trading profits, and if the business is being operated as a limited company, **corporation tax** will be paid on the trading profits.

We saw in Chapter 1 how the trading profits of an individual operating as a sole trader or in partnership are brought into an income tax computation for a tax year (6 April to 5 April). We will see how to bring the trading profits of a company into a corporation tax computation, in Chapter 6 of this Text.

Whether the business is unincorporated (sole trader or partnership) or incorporated (limited company) the tax computation will always start with the ADJUSTMENT OF PROFITS. **This is a vital area for all business types** and is the subject of this chapter. Many of the rules are the same for unincorporated businesses and for companies, with some differences highlighted in this chapter.

BADGES OF TRADE

Is a trade being carried on?

Firstly, it is important to understand whether an individual is in fact trading or not when he sells an item or items. If he is trading, the profits of that trade are subject to income tax. However, if a trade is not being carried on, any profit arising on the sale of an item may be exempt from tax or it may be subject to capital gains tax.

For example, a person who buys and sells stamps may be trading as a stamp dealer. Alternatively, stamp collecting may be a hobby of that person. In this case he is probably not trading.

The badges of trade

A trade is defined in legislation in a very unhelpful manner. Therefore it is left to the courts to provide guidance as to whether a trade exists or not. This guidance is summarised in a collection of principles known as the **'badges of trade'.**

The BADGES OF TRADE each provide evidence as to whether a trade is being carried on. The overall weight of the evidence determines the final decision. The badges of trade are:

The subject matter

Some items are commonly held as an **investment,** for example, works of art and antiques. A subsequent disposal may produce a gain of a capital nature rather

than a trading profit. However, where the subject matter of a transaction is such that it would not normally be held as an investment (for example, 1,000,000 rolls of toilet paper), it is presumed that any profit on resale is a trading profit.

The frequency of transactions

A series of similar transactions indicates trading. Conversely, a single transaction is unlikely to be considered as a trade.

The length of ownership

The purchase of items followed by sale soon afterwards indicates trading. Conversely, if items are held for a long time before sale there is less likely to be a trade.

Supplementary work and marketing

If work is done to make an asset more marketable, or steps are taken to find purchasers, there is likely to be a trade. For example, when a group of accountants bought, blended and recasked a quantity of brandy they were held to be taxable on a trading profit when the brandy was later sold.

A profit motive

If an item is bought with the intention of selling it at a profit, a trade is likely to exist.

The way in which an asset was acquired

If goods are acquired unintentionally, for example, by gift or inheritance, their later sale is unlikely to constitute trading.

The taxpayer's intentions

Where objective criteria clearly indicate that a trade is being carried on, the taxpayer's intentions are irrelevant. If, however, a transaction (objectively) has a dual purpose, you should consider the taxpayer's intentions. An example of a transaction with a dual purpose is the acquisition of a site partly as premises from which to conduct another trade, and partly with a view to possible development and resale of the site.

HOW IT WORKS

Tim is employed by an NHS trust as a medical consultant. In his spare time he buys and sells stamps. Tim regards this as a hobby and his only intention in acquiring stamps is to add them to his collection.

Tim attends stamp auctions several times a year to acquire stamps. Stamps are usually bought in lots of several stamps. Most stamps he adds to his collection and does not intend to sell. Stamps that he does not want to add to his collection he sells soon after purchase, usually at a profit.

Discuss whether or not Tim is trading with reference to the badges of trade.

We need to consider each of the badges of trade in turn:

The subject matter. Many people collect stamps as a hobby whilst stamp dealers trade in the purchase and sale of stamps. In this case this badge of trade does not help to decide the issue either way.

The frequency of transactions. Tim regularly attends stamp auctions to buy stamps and then often sells some of these. This frequency of purchasing and selling stamps may suggest that Tim trades in stamps.

The length of ownership. The fact that most stamps are added to Tim's collection and not sold (ie held for a long period of time) suggests that Tim is not trading.

Supplementary work and marketing. Tim does no supplementary work to the stamps and it is assumed that he does no marketing of the stamps he sells. As a result there is no indication that Tim is trading.

A profit motive. Although Tim buys and immediately sells some stamps at a profit, his main intention is to find stamps for his collection. This indicates that he is not trading.

The manner in which stamps were acquired. The fact that the stamps were bought rather than inherited or received by way of gift could indicate that Tim is trading.

It is the overall balance of the above evidence that determines whether a trade exists. On these facts it appears that Tim is not trading. Any profit on the sale of stamps could, however, be subject to capital gains tax.

ADJUSTMENT OF PROFITS

If it is decided that a trade does exist, the taxpayer (sole trader, partnership or limited company) will need to work out **taxable trading profits**.

This will be done by ADJUSTING THE ACCOUNTING PROFITS. **This is the starting point of the tax computation for all types of business.**

Taxable trading profits are not the same as the profits for the year shown in the accounts.

The trader arrives at the profit for the year in the accounts by taking income and deducting various trading expenses. However, the trader is unlikely to follow tax rules in arriving at this profit as, for example, there are some costs for which tax legislation does not allow a tax deduction, even though the taxpayer quite legitimately deducts them for accounting purposes.

Adjusting the profits for tax purposes

Therefore, the profit for the year in the accounts needs to be adjusted in order to arrive at the taxable trading profit.

Note that in the assessment the AAT may simply refer to this as the ADJUSTED TRADING PROFIT.

The rules for adjusting the accounting profits for tax purposes are broadly the same for both unincorporated and incorporated businesses, with a few specific differences that you need to be aware of. These differences are highlighted throughout this chapter.

The starting point for adjusting the profits for tax purposes is the **profit for the year in the statement of profit or loss**.

There are four types of adjustment to then consider:

(1) **Add back disallowable (non-deductible) expenditure.** This is EXPENDITURE that has been deducted in the accounts but that is not allowable for tax purposes. We will look at various types of disallowable expenditure below.

(2) **Deduct non-trading income.** This is INCOME that has been included in the accounts but which is not trading income. Examples include capital receipts and investment income (which is taxed separately to trading income) or income that is exempt from tax altogether.

(3) **Deduct allowable expenditure not included in accounts.** This consists of items that have not been deducted in the accounts but that tax law allows as a deduction from taxable trading profits. An example is CAPITAL ALLOWANCES which you will see in the next chapter of this Text.

(4) **Add income that must be taxed as trading income but that is not included in the accounts.** An example is where the trader takes goods from his business for his own use. For tax purposes you should treat this as though the trader sold those goods to himself for their MARKET VALUE. It is unlikely that the trader will have recorded this sale at market value in his accounts, so an adjustment will need to be made.

Task 1

Pratish trades as a car mechanic. His most recent accounts show a profit of £38,000. In arriving at this figure he deducted entertaining expenses of £2,000 and depreciation of £4,000. These amounts are not allowable for tax purposes. Capital allowances of £3,500 are available for tax purposes.

Using the pro forma layout provided, calculate the taxable trading profit. The starting figure has already been entered for you.

	£
Profit for the year in the accounts	38,000

CAPITAL AND REVENUE EXPENDITURE

In general, **revenue expenditure is the day to day expenditure** of the trade, for example lighting, heating, stationery and wages. **Capital expenditure relates to the acquisition or improvement of a capital asset** such as machinery or a shop.

When we are calculating **adjusted trading profits** it is important to distinguishing between revenue expenditure and capital expenditure as:

- **Revenue expenditure is broadly an allowable expense.**
- **Capital expenditure is broadly a disallowable expense** if it has been included in the statement of profit or loss (and other comprehensive income).

We will see in the next chapter of this Text, relief may be given for some types of capital expenditure through the capital allowances rules.

Task 2

Identify whether the following expenses are revenue or capital in nature by ticking the relevant box.

	Revenue	Capital
Paying employee wages	☐	☐
Paying rent for premises	☐	☐
Buying machinery	☐	☐
Buying a van	☐	☐
Building an extension to shop	☐	☐
Paying for repairs to car	☐	☐

Revenue expenditure

The distinction between capital and revenue expenditure can be a difficult one to make. The cost of repairing an asset is revenue expenditure but the cost of improving it is capital expenditure. The cost of repairs needed to put a newly acquired asset into a usable state is disallowable capital expenditure. However, the cost of repairs needed to remedy normal wear and tear on a newly acquired asset is allowable.

HOW IT WORKS

The cost of repairs needed to make a newly acquired ship seaworthy, before using it, is disallowable capital expenditure. However, if the ship had been seaworthy on acquisition the cost of making normal repairs would be allowable. This point was decided in a very famous case called *Law Shipping Co Ltd v CIR*.

You are not expected to remember case names for assessment purposes.

Task 3

A taxpayer bought a cinema that was usable on acquisition. However, the cinema was fairly dilapidated and various repairs were immediately carried out.

Decide whether the following statement is True or False.

The repairs are disallowable, being a capital expense.

	✓
True	
False	

ALLOWABLE AND DISALLOWABLE EXPENDITURE

You may see allowable and DISALLOWABLE EXPENDITURE referred to as deductible and non deductible expenditure. The two sets of terms are interchangeable.

The basic rule is that expenditure is allowable if it is **revenue** expenditure that is incurred WHOLLY AND EXCLUSIVELY FOR TRADE PURPOSES. If not, the expenditure is disallowable.

Wholly and exclusively for trade purposes

There is a case where a lady barrister incurred expenditure on black clothing to be worn in court. The expenditure was not deductible because it was not incurred exclusively for trade purposes. The expenditure had the dual purpose of allowing the barrister to be warmly and properly clad.

Strictly, expenditure incurred partly for private purposes and partly for business purposes has a dual purpose and is not deductible. However, HMRC sometimes allow taxpayers to apportion the expenditure between the part that is wholly for business purposes and therefore is deductible, and the part that is wholly for private purposes and therefore not deductible.

One important difference in the calculation of adjusted profits for companies is that there will **never be any adjustments for expenditure incurred for private purposes.** This is because the company itself cannot incur expenditure for private purposes. If however the company incurs expenditure for private purposes for its directors or employees the full amount is deductible for the company and the director or employee will be taxed as a benefit for income tax instead.

HOW IT WORKS

A sole trader who runs his business from home incurs £500 on heating and lighting bills. 30% of these bills relate to the business use of his house. £500 has been deducted in arriving at the accounts profit. How much should be added back in the calculation of taxable trading profits?

The 30% relating to business use is allowable. Therefore, 70% × £500 = £350 must be added back to the accounts profit as disallowable expenditure.

Task 4

Raj deducts his total motor expenses of £600 in calculating his accounts profit. 60% of Raj's motoring is for business purposes and 40% is for private purposes.

Calculate the amount of the motoring expenses that must be added back to the accounts profit in calculating taxable trading profits.

£	

Charitable donations

Donations to charity are not incidentally incurred in any trade. This means that they are not incurred for trade purposes and are therefore normally disallowable. However, where a donation is made to a small local charity, HMRC will allow the donation on the grounds that, in these circumstances, the donation is made to benefit the trade (through developing local goodwill etc).

Task 5

Norman, a greengrocer, deducts the following donations in computing his accounting profit:

£100 to Oxfam
£280 to a small local charity

Identify the total amount of the donations that must be added back in computing taxable trading profits.

Tick ONE box

Amount to add back	✓
£100	
£280	
£380	
None	

The treatment of various other items

The table below details various types of allowable and disallowable expenditure with mention of any differences between unincorporated businesses (sole traders and partnerships) and incorporated businesses (companies) where necessary.

Allowable expenditure	Disallowable expenditure	Comments
	Fines and penalties	HMRC usually allow parking fines incurred in parking an employee's car whilst on the employer's business. Fines relating to the owner of the business are, however, never allowed. Similarly, a company would not be able to deduct fines relating to directors
Costs of registering trade marks and patents		This is an exception to the rule of 'capital' related expenditure being disallowable
Incidental costs of obtaining loan finance		This deduction does not apply to companies because they get a deduction for the cost of borrowing in a different way. We look at this in chapter 6 of this Text
	Depreciation or amortisation	In specific circumstances a company can deduct these amounts, but this is outside the scope of this assessment
	Any salary or interest paid to a sole trader or partner	
	The private proportion of any expenses incurred by a sole trader or partner	The private proportion of a director's or employee's expenses is, however, deductible
Irrecoverable debts incurred in the course of a business. Specific provisions for irrecoverable debts (see below)	General provisions for irrecoverable debts (and other general provisions)	Loans to employees written off despite being specific are not allowable

Allowable expenditure	Disallowable expenditure	Comments
Patent and copyright royalties		Patent and copyright royalties paid for trade purposes are deductible
Staff entertaining	Non staff (eg customer) entertaining	
Gifts for employees Gifts to customers as long as they: ■ Cost no more than £50 per donee per year ■ They carry a conspicuous advertisement for the business ■ Are not food, drink, tobacco or vouchers exchangeable for such goods. Gifts to a small local charity if they benefit the trade	All other gifts including 'qualifying charitable donations'	Qualifying charitable donations are charitable gifts by companies on which tax relief is given. These are covered in Chapter 6 of this Text. The similar scheme relevant to individuals is not assessable in this Business Tax assessment.
Subscriptions to a professional or trade association	Political donations	Exceptionally, if it can be shown that political expenditure is incurred for the survival of the trade, then it is allowable
Legal and professional charges relating directly to the trade	Legal and professional charges relating to capital or non trading items	Deductible items include: ■ Charges incurred defending the taxpayer's title to non-current assets ■ Charges connected with an action for breach of contract

Allowable expenditure	Disallowable expenditure	Comments
	Accountancy expenses relating to specialist consultancy work	■ Expenses for the renewal (not the original grant) of a lease for less than 50 years ■ Charges for trade debt collection ■ Normal charges for preparing accounts and assisting with the self assessment of tax liabilities
Interest on loans taken out for trade purposes	Interest on overdue tax	These rules are for unincorporated businesses. Companies have different rules for interest. We look at these in Chapter 6 of this Text
Costs of seconding employees to charities or educational establishments		
Expenditure incurred in the seven years prior to the commencement of a trade		Provided expenditure is of a type that would have been allowed had the trade started. Treat as an expense on the first day of trading
Removal expenses (to new business premises)		Only if not an expansionary move
Travelling expenses on the trader's business	Travel from home to the trader's place of business	

Allowable expenditure	Disallowable expenditure	Comments
Redundancy payments		If the trade ceases, the limit on allowability is 3 × the statutory amount (in addition to the statutory amount)
	15% of leasing costs of car with CO_2 emissions in excess of 130g/km	

Irrecoverable debts

Only irrecoverable debts incurred wholly and exclusively for the purposes of the trade are deductible for taxation purposes. Thus loans to employees written off are not deductible unless the business is that of making loans, or it can be shown that the write off was earnings paid out for the benefit of the trade.

A review of trade receivables may be carried out to assess their fair value, and any irrecoverable debts written off. As a specific provision, this is an allowable expense and therefore no adjustment is needed.

Accounting rules are such that it is unlikely that any general provisions will be seen in practice. An example would be if a trader estimates a percentage of his trade receivables (rather than specific amounts relating to specific customers) to be irrecoverable. In the event that general provisions do arise, increases or decreases in a general provision are not allowable and an adjustment is needed. Let's have a look at the following example of an irrecoverable debts account:

HOW IT WORKS

IRRECOVERABLE DEBTS ACCOUNT

The account below results in a credit to the statement of profit or loss of £124. What adjustment should be made to the profit **for the year** when calculating taxable trading profits?

2014	£	£	*2014*	£	£
			1 January		
			Provisions b/d		
			General	150	
			Specific	381	
					531
Provisions c/d					
General	207				
Specific	200				
		407			
Statement of profit or loss		124			
		531			531
			2015		
			1 January		
			Provisions b/d		407

The only adjustment you need to consider is the increase in general provision from £150 to £207. Thus £57 is added to the accounts profit to arrive at taxable profit.

Task 6

Fish Ltd has an accounts profit of £180,000 after charging legal expenses as follows:

	£
Expenses relating to purchase of new offices	7,000
Expenses relating to employee service contracts	2,000
Expenses relating to the renewal of a 25 year lease	1,500

Calculate how much must be added back in computing taxable trading profits.

Tick ONE box

Amount to add back	✓
£7,000	
£9,000	
£10,500	
£8,500	

Task 7

A sole trader charged the following expenses in computing his accounts profit:

	£
Fine for breach of Factories Act	1,000
Cost of specialist tax consultancy work	2,000
Redundancy payments	10,000
Salary for himself	15,000
Leasing cost of car (CO_2 emissions 150g/km)	3,000

The redundancy payments were made for trade purposes as a result of reorganisation of the business. The trade is continuing.

Calculate how much must be added back in computing taxable trading profits.

Tick ONE box

Amount to add back	✓
£17,450	
£16,000	
£18,450	
£11,450	

Task 8

Sana runs her business from home. Sana has deducted all of her heating and lighting bills of £800 in computing her accounts profit. 30% of the heating and lighting bills relate to the business. The amount that must be added back in computing taxable trading profits is:

£ [   ]

Task 9

Decide whether each of the items in the entertainment account below should be added back in computing taxable trading profits.

Expenditure	£	Add back ✓
Staff tennis outing for 30 employees	1,800	
2,000 tee shirts with firm's logo given to race runners	4,500	
Advertising and sponsorship of an athletic event	2,000	
Entertaining customers	7,300	
Staff Christmas party (30 employees)	2,400	

Task 10

Here is the statement of profit or loss for Mr Pring, a trader.

	£	£
Gross profit from operations		60,000
Rental income received		860
		60,860
Wages and salaries	27,000	
Rent and rates	2,000	
Depreciation charge	1,500	
Specific irrecoverable debts written off	150	
Provision against a fall in the price of raw materials	5,000	
Entertainment expenses	750	
Patent royalties	1,200	
Bank interest	300	
Legal expenses on acquisition of new factory	250	
		(38,150)
Profit for the year		22,710

(a) Salaries include £3,500 paid to Mrs Pring who works full time in the business.

(b) No staff were entertained.

(c) The provision of £5,000 is a general provision charged because of an anticipated trade recession.

Using the proforma layout provided, compute the taxable trading profit.

	£	£

SELF EMPLOYMENT TAX RETURN PAGE

A copy of the page you may have to complete is available at the end of this chapter. AAT have confirmed that this is the only page you should expect to see from the self assessment tax return. You will notice that the boxes on the left side of the return show all of a trader's expenses and the boxes on the right hand side highlight which of those expenses are disallowable for tax purposes. For example if a trader has a depreciation charge of £500, this will be shown in both box 29 and box 44.

You will be able to practise completing this form in the Business Tax Question Bank.

Assessment focus

None of the information in this chapter is included within the 'Taxation Data' which you will be provided with in the live assessment.

The information included in this chapter typically will be tested in the following tasks:

Task 1 – Computation of adjusted profits for sole traders, partnerships and limited companies

Task 8 – Tax returns

Performance feedback

The feedback given below relates to students' performance on the AQ2010 version of the assessments. However, the points made by the assessor will be equally as valid for students sitting the assessment under AQ2013.

Task 1.1 (AQ2010)

This task is meant to be a basic question that allows students to settle into the assessment, and will tend to be either multi choice or true/false style. It mainly involves badges of trade and the distinction between capital and revenue expenditure. The results are showing that students are not performing as well in this task as would be expected, and there is evidence that the question is not being read carefully.

Task 1.2 (AQ2010)

The vast majority of students illustrated a lack of detailed knowledge not knowing if interest received in the accounts should be added back or deducted.

Task 2.10 (AQ2010)

The second page from the self-employment tax return is quite straightforward to complete but there are three things to watch out for: ensure that the disallowed amount is entered in the box adjacent to the relevant box on the left hand side.

Some students simply put the disallowed amounts in the first five or so boxes from the top, hence gaining no marks. To get the mark, students must input the right amount into the right box. The second thing to watch for is to not forget to disallow the depreciation that is shown in box 29, and lastly, don't forget to add a total in box 46.

CHAPTER OVERVIEW

- The badges of trade give guidance whether or not a trade is being carried on

- Revenue expenses are generally allowable expenses for computing taxable trading profits but capital expenses are not (unless relieved through capital allowances- see next chapter)

- The main disallowable items that you must add back in computing taxable trading profits are:
    - Entertaining (other than staff entertaining)
    - Depreciation charges (deduct capital allowances instead)
    - Increase in general provisions
    - Fines
    - Legal fees relating to capital items
    - Wages or salary paid to a business owner
    - The private proportion of any expenses for a sole trader/partner (not applicable to a company)

- Deduct non trading income/capital profits included in the accounts from the accounts profit to arrive at taxable trading profits

Keywords

Badges of trade – indicate whether or not a trade is being carried on

Adjustment of profits – is the adjustment of the accounting profits to comply with tax legislation

Disallowable expenditure – is expenditure that cannot be deducted in computing taxable trading profit

Expenditure wholly and exclusively for trade purposes – is expenditure that is incidental to the trade and that does not have a dual purpose

TEST YOUR LEARNING

Test 1

Which of the following expenses are allowable when computing taxable trading profits?

	Allowable ✓
Legal fees incurred on the acquisition of a factory to be used for trade purposes	
Heating for factory	
Legal fees incurred on pursuing trade receivables	
Acquiring a machine to be used in the factory	

Test 2

A sole trader incurs the following expenditure on entertaining and gifts

	£
Staff entertaining	700
50 Christmas food hampers given to customers	240
Entertaining customers	900
	1,840

How much of the above expenditure is allowable for tax purposes?

£ [   ]

Test 3

For each of the following expenses, show whether they are allowable or disallowable by ticking the relevant boxes.

	Allowable	Disallowable
Parking fines incurred by the owner of the business	☐	☐
Parking fines incurred by an employee whilst on the employer's business	☐	☐
Parking fines incurred by the director of a company whilst on company business	☐	☐
Legal costs incurred in relation to acquiring a 10 year lease of property for the first time	☐	☐
Legal costs incurred in relation to the renewal of a lease for 20 years.	☐	☐
Gifts of calendars to customers, costing £4 each and displaying an advertisement for the company	☐	☐
Gifts of bottles of whisky to customers, costing £12 each	☐	☐

Test 4

Herbert, a self-employed carpenter, makes various items of garden furniture for sale. He takes a bird table from stock and sets it up in his own garden. The cost of making the bird table amounts to £80, and Herbert would normally expect to achieve a mark-up of 20% on such goods.

Identify the adjustment Herbert needs to make to the accounts for tax purposes, assuming he has reflected in the accounts the deduction for the cost of making the table.

Tick ONE box.

	✓
£80 must be deducted from the accounts profit	
£80 must be added back to the accounts profit	
£96 must be deducted from the accounts profit	
£96 must be added back to the accounts profit	

Test 5

Set out below is the irrecoverable debts account of Kingfisher, a sole trader:

IRRECOVERABLE DEBTS

	£		£
		1.4.14	
		Provisions b/d	
		General	2,500
		Specific (trade)	1,875
31.3.15			
Provisions c/d			
General	1,800		
Specific (trade)	4,059	Statement of profit	1,484
		or loss	
	5,859		5,859

Insert the amount that needs adjusting and tick whether it should be added to or deducted from Kingfisher's accounts profit to arrive at taxable trading profits.

£	
Added back ✓	**Deducted** ✓

Test 6

Trude works from home as a self employed hairdresser. She incurs £450 on heating and lighting bills and this amount is deducted in her accounts. 20% of this expenditure relates to the business use of her home.

How much of the expenditure is disallowable for tax purposes?

£	

EXTRACT FROM SELF-EMPLOYMENT TAX RETURN

Business expenses

Please read the *Self-employment (full) notes* before filling in this section.

Total expenses	Disallowable expenses
If your annual turnover was below £81,000 you may just put your total expenses in box 31	Use this column if the figures in boxes 17 to 30 include disallowable amounts

	Total expenses		Disallowable expenses
17	Cost of goods bought for resale or goods used	32	
	£ · 0 0		£ · 0 0
18	Construction industry – *payments to subcontractors*	33	
	£ · 0 0		£ · 0 0
19	Wages, salaries and other staff costs	34	
	£ · 0 0		£ · 0 0
20	Car, van and travel expenses	35	
	£ · 0 0		£ · 0 0
21	Rent, rates, power and insurance costs	36	
	£ · 0 0		£ · 0 0
22	Repairs and renewals of property and equipment	37	
	£ · 0 0		£ · 0 0
23	Phone, fax, stationery and other office costs	38	
	£ · 0 0		£ · 0 0
24	Advertising and business entertainment costs	39	
	£ · 0 0		£ · 0 0
25	Interest on bank and other loans	40	
	£ · 0 0		£ · 0 0
26	Bank, credit card and other financial charges	41	
	£ · 0 0		£ · 0 0
27	Irrecoverable debts written off	42	
	£ · 0 0		£ · 0 0
28	Accountancy, legal and other professional fees	43	
	£ · 0 0		£ · 0 0
29	Depreciation and loss/profit on sale of assets	44	
	£ · 0 0		£ · 0 0
30	Other business expenses	45	
	£ · 0 0		£ · 0 0
31	Total expenses (total of boxes 17 to 30)	46	Total disallowable expenses (total of boxes 32 to 45)
	£ · 0 0		£ · 0 0

BPP LEARNING MEDIA

chapter 3:
CAPITAL ALLOWANCES

chapter coverage 📖

Capital allowances give tax relief to businesses which invest in certain capital assets. We look at the availability of allowances for both unincorporated and incorporated businesses and how to calculate these allowances. The chapter concludes with the differences between unincorporated and incorporated businesses, although this will be reinforced in later chapters.

The topics that we shall cover are:

- ✍ Basic principles
- ✍ Annual investment allowance (AIA)
- ✍ First year allowance
- ✍ The main pool
  - Writing down allowance
  - Disposals
  - Periods that are not 12 months long
  - The cessation of a business
- ✍ Assets not included in the main pool
  - Cars with CO_2 emissions in excess of 130g/km
  - Assets used partly for private purposes
  - Short life assets
- ✍ Differences between unincorporated and incorporated businesses

INTRODUCTION

In the last chapter we learnt the importance of distinguishing between capital expenditure and revenue expenditure. We saw that revenue expenditure is generally an allowable expense when computing trading income but capital expenditure is not.

Instead there is a system of CAPITAL ALLOWANCES that gives tax relief for some types of expenditure on capital assets.

Having adjusted the accounting profits for tax purposes as we saw in Chapter 2, including adding back any depreciation, **capital allowances** are then given as the final deduction to arrive at taxable trading profits.

Capital allowances are available to both unincorporated and incorporated businesses in broadly the same way. Important differences are highlighted below within this Chapter.

Task 1

Identify whether the following are allowable (revenue based) or disallowable (capital based).

	Allowable (revenue based) ✓	Disallowable (capital based) ✓
Rent paid on premises		
Purchase of an office		
Purchase of machinery		
Repairs to machinery		
Redecoration of premises		
Depreciation charge on machinery		

Not all capital expenditure qualifies for capital allowances.

Expenditure on PLANT AND MACHINERY qualifies for capital allowances. For this purpose machinery is given its ordinary everyday meaning, plant, however, is harder to define.

The main description of PLANT is that **plant is apparatus that performs a job in the business. Apparatus that is merely part of the setting of the business is not plant.** For example expenditure on cars, vans and furniture would qualify for

capital allowances, as they perform a function (or job) in the business, but walls or ceilings in a retail premises would not as they are part of the setting.

Assessment focus

The AAT have advised us that theory on what is, and what is not plant and machinery is not necessary for the Business Tax assessment.

BASIC PRINCIPLES

The main pool

Most expenditure on plant and machinery is put into a pool of assets known as the **main pool**. This includes expenditure on cars with CO_2 emissions of 130g/km or less.

Writing Down Allowances

Capital allowances known as WRITING DOWN ALLOWANCES (see below) are claimed on the balance of expenditure in the pool for each period. This is done on a reducing balance basis, after adding in current period additions and deducting the proceeds of current period disposals. The balance of expenditure remaining in the pool after allowances are claimed, is carried forward to the next period.

Before we look at writing down allowances in detail, we look at a special type of allowance, the annual investment allowance, which was introduced to encourage businesses to invest in plant and machinery.

ANNUAL INVESTMENT ALLOWANCE (AIA)

From 1 April 2014 (6 April 2014 for unincorporated businesses) a business can claim an ANNUAL INVESTMENT ALLOWANCE (AIA), giving 100% tax relief on the first £500,000 of expenditure on plant and machinery in a 12 month PERIOD OF ACCOUNT. The period of account is the period for which the business prepares its accounts. **The AIA is not available for expenditure on cars.**

HOW IT WORKS

Kieran starts a business on 6 April 2014 and makes up his first set of accounts to 5 April 2015. He buys the following items of plant and machinery.

		£
12 April 2014	Office equipment	2,000
13 May 2014	Delivery van	15,000
1 August 2014	Car for salesman, CO2 emissions 125g/km	14,000
2 December 2014	Machine for workshop	87,000

The amount of the annual investment allowance that Kieran can claim is:

		£
12 April 2014	Office equipment	2,000
13 May 2014	Delivery van	15,000
2 December 2014	Machine for workshop	87,000
AIA for y/end 5 April 2015 (less than £500,000)		104,000

The AIA cannot be used against the cost of the car. Note that the AIA is available against the cost of the delivery van, however.

If Kieran had expenditure on plant and machinery of more than £500,000 the excess expenditure would go into the main pool (along with the expenditure on the car) and writing down allowances could be claimed on it.

Task 2

Jojo Ltd has been trading for many years, making up accounts to 31 March each year. In the year to 31 March 2015 the company incurs the following capital expenditure:

		£
14 May 2014	Computer system	27,000
12 July 2014	Machinery for factory	150,000
12 September 2014	Factory extension	217,000
17 November 2014	Motor car for director	88,000

(1) Tick for which of these items Jojo Ltd can claim the Annual Investment Allowance

	Claim	Not claim
Computer system	☐	☐
Machinery for factory	☐	☐
Factory extension	☐	☐
Motor car for director	☐	☐

(2) The maximum AIA that Jojo Ltd can claim is:

£ _____

Increase to the annual investment allowance

For expenditure **prior to 1 April (6 April for unincorporated businesses) 2014** the most recent level of AIA was **£250,000 per annum**.

Where an accounting period **straddles the 1/6 April 2014** (for both unincorporated and incorporated businesses) the maximum AIA available for the accounting period is calculated by **pro-rating the relevant AIA limits** for the number of months in the accounting period that fall either side of 1/6 April 2014.

Assessment focus

The rules for calculating the maximum AIA available for periods straddling 1/6 April 2014 are slightly more complex than we have shown below. However the AAT have advised us that the full complexity of this will not be needed and tasks in the Business Tax assessment will be designed to accommodate this.

HOW IT WORKS

A business makes up it accounts to 30 September each year. For the year end 30 September 2014 the AIA would firstly need to be prorated between the six months prior to 1/6 April 2014 and the six months falling after 1/6 April 2014 as follows:

- £250,000 × 6/12 = **£125,000** – For period prior to 1/6 April 2014
- £500,000 × 6/12 = **£250,000** – For period from 1/6 April 2014

The **maximum AIA available for the year end 30 September 2014** is therefore £125,000 + £250,000 = **£375,000.**

Task 3

Mr Blonde (a sole trader) has the following expenditure on plant in his year end 31 December 2014:

January 2014 – £55,000

May 2014 – £300,000

Complete the following statements.

The maximum AIA available for the year to 31 December 2014 is

£	

The maximum AIA that Mr Blonde can claim for the year to 31 December 2014 is

£	

Task 4

Orange Ltd has the following expenditure on plant in its year end 30 June 2014:

April 2014 – £450,000

Complete the following statements.

The maximum AIA available for the year to 30 June 2014 is

£	

The maximum AIA that Mr Orange can claim for the year to 30 June 2014 is

£	

FIRST YEAR ALLOWANCE

A **100% first year allowance** is available in the period in which expenditure is incurred on:

(a) Cars with CO_2 emissions not exceeding 95g/km (low emission cars) or electrically propelled

(b) Energy saving and water efficient plant

HOW IT WORKS

Ruby started business as a sole trader on 1 October 2013 and made up her first set of accounts to 30 September 2014.

In the year to 30 September 2014, Ruby bought the following assets:

9 October 2013	Plant	£10,000
10 May 2014	Machinery	£106,000
13 July 2014	Car (CO_2 emissions 85g/km)	£7,000

The **maximum AIA** is therefore calculated as follows:

- £125,000 (250,000 × 6/12) + £250,000 (500,000 × 6/12) = **£375,000** – for the whole accounting period

The capital allowances available to Ruby in the year to 30 September 2014 are:

	AIA £	FYA @ 100% £	Main pool £	Allowances £
y/e 30 Sept 2014				
AIA only additions				
Plant	10,000			
Machinery	106,000			
AIA (max 375,000)	(116,000)			116,000
Balance to transfer to main pool	0		0	
FYA @ 100% addition				
Low emission car		7,000		
FYA @ 100%		(7,000)		7,000
Balance to transfer to main pool		(0)	0	
C/f			0	
Capital allowances				123,000

THE MAIN POOL

Writing down allowance (WDA)

A WRITING DOWN ALLOWANCE (WDA) is given on the main pool at the rate of 18% a year (on a reducing balance basis). As mentioned above, the WDA is calculated on the value of pooled plant, after adding current period additions and taking out current period disposals (as explained shortly).

The additions will include:

■ Expenditure that qualifies for the AIA but is in excess of the maximum AIA available for the period.

■ Cars with CO_2 emissions between 96g/km and 130g/km. These are cars that do not qualify for 100% FYA and do not go into the special rate pool (see later).

HOW IT WORKS

On 6 April 2014 Panikah has a balance on his main pool of plant and machinery of £28,000. In the year to 5 April 2015 he bought a car with CO_2 emissions of 120g/km for £10,000. He also sold a machine for £2,000. The capital allowances available for the year are:

	Main pool £	Allowances
B/f	28,000	
Addition (no AIA on car)	10,000	
Less disposal	(2,000)	
	36,000	
WDA @ 18%	(6.480)	6,480
C/f	29,520	

Task 5

Nitin has a balance of £10,000 brought forward on 6 April 2014 on his main pool of plant and machinery. In the year to 5 April 2015 he bought a car with CO_2 emissions of 105g/km for £8,000 and disposed of an asset for £6,000.

Calculate the capital allowances available on the main pool.

HOW IT WORKS

Julius Ltd makes up accounts to 31 March each year. At 1 April 2014, the value carried forward in its main pool is £20,000.

In the year to 31 March 2015, Julius Ltd bought the following assets:

1 April 2014	Machine	£495,000
12 October 2014	Van	£17,500
10 January 2015	Car for salesman	£19,000
	(CO_2 emissions 115g/km)	

The company disposed of plant on 15 Sept 2014 for proceeds of £12,000.

The maximum capital allowances that Julius Ltd can claim for the year ended 31 March 2015 are:

	AIA £	Main pool £	Allowances £
Y/e 31 March 2015			
B/f		20,000	
AIA additions			
1.4.14 Machine	495,000		
12.10.14 Van	17,500		
	512,500		
AIA	(500,000)		500,000
	12,500		
Transfer to main pool	(12,500)	12,500	
Non AIA additions			
10.1.15 Car		19,000	
Disposal			
15.9.14 Plant		(12,000)	
		39,500	
WDA @ 18%		(7,110)	7,110
C/f		32,390	
Maximum capital allowances			507,110

Note the layout of this computation and the order in which the figures are entered. It is important to transfer the excess amount remaining after applying the AIA to the main pool as this excess is entitled to the normal WDA of 18%.

Task 6

Mr White has a balance of £12,000 brought forward on 6 April 2014 on his main pool of plant and machinery. In the year to 5 April 2015 he bought a machine for £488,000 and furniture for £21,000.

Calculate the capital allowances available to Mr White for the year ended 5 April 2015.

Disposals

As you have seen above, the most common disposal value at which assets are entered in a capital allowances computation is the sale proceeds. However, there is an overriding rule that the capital allowances disposal value cannot exceed the original purchase price of the asset. Try applying this rule in the following Task.

Task 7

On 6 April 2014, a sole trader had a balance on his main pool of £47,000. Plant that had cost £7,000 was sold for proceeds of £14,000 on 1 August 2014.

Calculate the maximum capital allowances available on this main pool for the year to 5 April 2015.

Periods that are not 12 months long

The annual investment allowance and the writing down allowance are adjusted by the fraction months/12:

(a) For unincorporated businesses where the period of account is longer or shorter than 12 months.

(b) For companies where the accounting period is shorter than 12 months (a company's accounting period for tax purposes is never longer than 12 months). We will see what is meant by an accounting period when we look at the construction of a corporation tax computation in Chapter 6 of this Text.

The 100% first year allowance is not adjusted for periods of account shorter or longer than 12 months.

HOW IT WORKS

Melissa had a value brought forward on her main pool of plant and machinery on 6 April 2014 of £40,000.

She prepared accounts for the nine months to 31 December 2014.

Melissa's maximum capital allowances for this period, assuming there were no disposals or additions are computed as follows:

9 m/e 31 December 2014	Main pool	Allowances
	£	£
B/f	40,000	
WDA × 18% × 9/12	(5,400)	5,400
C/f	34,600	

Melissa's maximum capital allowances for the period are £5,400.

In this example, the capital allowances would have been exactly the same if this had related to a company, rather than Melissa.

Task 8

Gotaum had a tax written down value brought forward on his main pool of plant and machinery on 1 January 2015 of £20,000. He prepared accounts for the three months to 31 March 2015. During this period he bought a car with CO_2 emissions of 120g/km for £4,000.

Compute Gotaum's capital allowances, assuming there were no disposals in the period.

HOW IT WORKS

Oscar, a sole trader, makes up accounts for the 18 months to 31 December 2015. The brought forward value on his main pool on 1 July 2014 was £81,000. He bought the following assets:

10 July 2014	Plant	£210,000
10 October 2014	Car for salesman	
	(CO_2 emissions 90g/km)	£11,000
12 August 2015	Plant	£550,000

The capital allowances claim (assuming rates remain unchanged) that Oscar can make for the period ended 31 December 2015 is calculated as follows:

	AIA £	Main pool £	Allowances £
18 m/e 31 December 2015			
B/f		81,000	
AIA acquisition			
10.7.14 Plant	210,000		
12.8.15 Plant	550,000		
AIA £500,000 × 18/12	(750,000)		750,000
	10,000		
Transfer balance to pool	(10,000)	10,000	
FYA acquisition			
10.10.14 Car	11,000		
FYA @ 100%	(11,000)		11,000
		91,000	
WDA @ 18% × 18/12		(24,570)	24,570
C/f		66,430	
Allowances			785,570

Note: The AIA and WDA are scaled up for the eighteen month period, whereas the FYA is never scaled up or down.

This working would not be the same had it related to a company, as the eighteen month period would be split into two accounting periods (a 12 month period and a six month period). We look at accounting periods for companies later in the Text.

Task 9

Marie has been trading for many years, making up her accounts to 30 April. The value of her main pool on 30 April 2014 was £12,000.

She then decided to make up her accounts to 31 December and made up accounts for the eight month period to 31 December 2014. In this period she bought the following assets:

14 June 2014	Office furniture	£135,000
15 August 2014	Machinery	£255,000

What is the capital allowances claim that Marie can make for the period ended 31 December 2014?

The cessation of a business

When a business stops trading, **no AIA, WDAs or FYAs are given in the final period of account** (unincorporated businesses) or accounting period (companies).

Additions in the final period are added to the pool in the normal way. Similarly, any disposal proceeds (limited to cost) of assets sold in the final period are deducted from the balance of qualifying expenditure. If assets are not sold they are deemed to be disposed of on the final day of trading for their market value. For example a sole trader may keep a car from the business that has just ceased trading and so must deduct the market value from the pool.

If, after the above adjustments, a positive balance of qualifying expenditure remains in the pool then a BALANCING ALLOWANCE equal to this amount is given. **The balancing allowance is deducted from taxable trading profits.** If on the other hand the balance on the pool has become negative, a BALANCING CHARGE equal to the negative amount is given. **The balancing charge increases taxable trading profits.**

Balancing allowances on the main pool and the special rate pool (see below) can only arise on cessation of trade, whereas balancing charges on these pools, although most commonly happen on cessation can arise whilst trade is still in progress.

HOW IT WORKS

The balance of expenditure on Rogue Ltd's main pool of plant and machinery was £40,000 on 30 June 2014. Rogue Ltd stopped trading on 31 December 2014. All assets in the main pool were sold on 31 December 2014 for £25,000.

Assuming that all assets were sold for less than their original cost, the balancing allowance or balancing charge arising in the final period is:

	Main pool	Allowances
	£	£
B/f	40,000	
Less disposal proceeds	(25,000)	
	15,000	
Balancing allowance	(15,000)	15,000

The balancing allowance is deducted in arriving at taxable trading profits.

ASSETS NOT INCLUDED IN THE MAIN POOL

We have seen above how to compute capital allowances on the main pool of plant and machinery. However, some special items are not put into the main pool. A separate record of allowances must be kept for these assets.

Assets that are not included in the main pool are:

(a) Cars with CO_2 emissions in excess of 130g/km

(b) Assets not wholly used for business purposes in **unincorporated businesses** (such as cars with private use by the proprietor)

(c) Short-life assets for which an election has been made (see below)

We will look at each of these assets in turn.

Cars with CO_2 emissions in excess of 130g/km

Cars with CO_2 emissions in excess of 130g/km are put in a pool known as the SPECIAL RATE POOL. The **WDA rate on the special rate pool is 8% for a 12 month period** calculated on the pool balance (after any additions and disposals) at the end of the chargeable period.

HOW IT WORKS

Jason is a sole trader making up accounts to 30 November each year. The brought forward balance on his special rate pool on 1 December 2013 was £9,000. On 10 April 2014 Jason bought a car for £11,000 with CO_2 emissions of 165g/km. The car was used solely for business purposes.

The capital allowances available for the year to 30 November 2014 are:

	Special rate pool £	Allowances £
y/e 30 November 2014		
B/f	9,000	
Addition	11,000	
	20,000	
WDA @ 8%	(1,600)	1,600
C/F	18,400	
Capital allowances		1,600

Task 10

Hermione commenced trading on 6 June 2014 and prepared her first accounts for the ten months to 5 April 2015. She bought a car with CO_2 emissions of 180 g/km for use in her business on 12 January 2015 for £18,000. Show the capital allowances available to Hermione in the ten months to 5 April 2015.

Assets used partly for private purposes

An asset (for example, a car) that is used partly for PRIVATE PURPOSES by a sole trader or a partner is never put in the main pool or special rate pool. You should put the asset in a pool of its own.

Capital allowances are calculated on the full cost. However, only the business use proportion of the allowances is allowed as a deduction from trading profits. This restriction applies to the AIA, FYAs, WDAs, balancing allowances and balancing charges.

Note that when an individual asset is held in a pool of its own a balancing allowance or charge will always arise at the date of disposal.

An asset with some private use by an employee (not the business owner), suffers no restriction. The employee may be taxed on a benefit, so the business is entitled to full capital allowances on such assets. This means **there is never any private use restriction in a company's capital allowance computation** whether the asset is used by an employee or director.

HOW IT WORKS

On 1 August 2014 a sole trader, who has been in business for many years, making up accounts to 5 April, buys a car with CO_2 emissions of 120g/km for £7,000. The private use proportion is 10%. He sells it for £2,000 on 15 February 2017.

The capital allowances for the three years to 5 April 2017 are computed as follows:

	Private use car £		Allowances 90% £
Y/e 5 April 2015			
Purchase price	7,000		
WDA 18% of £7,000 = £1,260	(1,260)	× 90%	1,134
	5,740		
Y/e 5 April 2016			
WDA @ 18%	(1,033)	× 90%	930
	4,707		
Y/e 5 April 2017			
Proceeds	(2,000)		
Balancing Allowance	2,707	× 90%	2,436

Note that full allowances are deducted in the private use asset column but the allowances (in the allowances column) to be deducted in computing taxable trading profits are restricted to the business proportion of the allowances.

Note that the car was bought for £7,000 and sold for £2,000, costing the business £5,000. However the trader is only entitled to allowances for the 90% business use of £4,500 (£5,000 × 90%). You can see over the three years of ownership the sole trader claimed £(1,134 + 930 + 2,436) = £4,500.

If the car had emissions in excess of 130 g/km, the WDA would have been given at the rate of 8%.

Task 11

Pippa, a sole trader, bought a car with CO_2 emissions of 165g/km on 1 June 2014 for £20,000. She uses the car 75% for business purposes. Pippa makes up accounts to 5 April each year.

Show the capital allowances on the car for the year ended 5 April 2015.

Short life assets

A SHORT LIFE ASSET is an asset that a trader expects to dispose of within **eight years** of the end of the period of acquisition.

A trader can make a DEPOOLING ELECTION to keep such an asset in its own individual pool. **The advantage of this is that a balancing allowance can be given when the asset is disposed of**. Such an election would not be made if the asset is entitled to 100% FYA or AIA.

For an unincorporated business, the time limit for electing is the 31 January that is 22 months after the end of the tax year in which the period of account of the

expenditure ends. (For a company, it is two years after the end of the accounting period of the expenditure.)

If the asset is disposed of within eight years of the end of the period of account or accounting period in which it was bought, a balancing charge or allowance is made on its disposal. However, if the asset is not disposed of within this period, the tax written down value is transferred to the main pool at the end of that period. Short life asset treatment cannot be claimed for:

- Motor cars
- Plant used partly for private purposes

The AIA can be used against short life assets but it is more tax efficient to use it against expenditure that would fall into the main pool.

DIFFERENCES BETWEEN UNINCORPORATED AND INCORPORATED BUSINESSES

Throughout this chapter we have seen that the rules for calculating capital allowances are broadly the same for all types of business.

Two important differences in the calculation of capital allowances are as follows:

- There is never a **private use asset** column in a company's capital allowance computation. This is because there is never any reduction of allowances to take account of any private use of an asset. The director or employee suffers a taxable benefit instead.

- Companies deal with a long **period of account** (accounts that have been made up for more than 12 months) in a different way to individuals or partnerships, which has an impact on the capital allowance computations.

Individuals work out capital allowances for the period of account, whether it be longer or shorter than 12 months.

Companies with a period of account longer than 12 months have to split it into two accounting periods and will then do a capital allowances computation for each accounting period.

This will be reinforced in Chapter 4 for unincorporated businesses and Chapter 6 for incorporated businesses.

Assessment focus

In the live assessment you will be provided with 'Taxation Data' that can be accessed through pop up windows. The content of these taxation data tables has been reproduced at the front of this Text.

The rates of all the allowances covered in this chapter are included within 'taxation data 1', along with the limits for the annual investment allowance. Make sure you familiarise yourself with the content and practise referring to it as you work through this Text.

The information included in this chapter typically will be tested in the following task:

Task 2 – Computation of capital allowances for sole traders, partnerships and limited companies

Performance feedback

The feedback given below relates to students' performance on the AQ2010 version of the assessments. However, the points made by the assessor will be equally as valid for students who will be sitting the assessment under AQ2013.

Task 1.7 (AQ2010)

'Students can expect a range of situations such as sole traders, partnerships, limited companies, long and short periods of account, opening businesses and closing businesses.

Students generally learn this topic well and only one fifth of all students failed to meet the required standard, and another fifth gained full marks.

Aside from small errors that might be expected in questions of this size, such as deducting private usage in limited company situations, the most recurring error was in the inability to handle periods of less, or more than, 12 months. Whilst many students may time apportion the annual investment allowance, they fail to also adjust the written down allowance. Equally common is computing a long period of account for a limited company in the same way that this would be handled for a sole trader.

Also, students must spend more time on handling the situation where a business ceases to trade. In questions of this nature, the vast majority of students will apply WDA before deducting the proceeds or market value from the pools.'

CHAPTER OVERVIEW

- Assets that perform a function in the trade are generally plant. Assets that are part of the setting are not plant

- Most expenditure on plant and machinery goes into the main pool

- An annual investment allowance (AIA) of £500,000 from 1/6 April 2014, is available on expenditure other than cars. The limit is prorated for periods of more or less than 12 months long

- FYAs at 100% are available on low emission cars and energy and water saving plant

- There is a writing down allowance (WDA) of 18% on the balance of the main pool in a 12 month period

- WDAs are time apportioned in short or long periods

- FYAs are never time apportioned for short or long periods

- Balancing allowances or balancing charges will given when the trade ceases, and when an asset is disposed of which is not included in the main pool or special rate pool

- Private use assets by sole traders and partners have restricted capital allowances

- An election can be made to depool short life assets. If a depooled asset is not sold within eight years of the end of the period of acquisition, the value of the short life asset at the end of that period is transferred to the main pool

- Cars are dealt with according to their CO_2 emissions:

  Up to 95g/km – FYA at 100%

  96g/km to 130g/km – main pool with WDA of 18%

  Above 130g/km – special rate pool with WDA of 8%

Keywords

Plant – is apparatus that performs a function in the business. Apparatus that is merely part of the setting is not plant

An **Annual Investment Allowance (AIA)** – is available in a period in which expenditure is incurred on plant and machinery

A **Writing Down Allowance (WDA)** – is a capital allowance of 18% per annum given on the main pool of plant and machinery or 8% per annum on the balance in the special rate pool

A **First Year Allowance (FYA)** – Available at 100% on low emission cars and certain energy saving and water efficient plant

A **balancing allowance** – is given when a positive balance remains at cessation or disposal of certain assets

A **balancing charge** – is given when a negative balance remains at cessation or disposal of certain assets

A **private use asset** – has restricted capital allowances but does not apply to companies

A **short life asset** – is an asset that a trader expects to dispose of within eight years of the end of the period of acquisition

A **depooling election** – is an election not to put an asset into the main pool of plant and machinery

The **period of account** – is the period for which a business prepares its accounts

TEST YOUR LEARNING

Test 1

An item of plant is acquired for £2,000 and sold five years later for £3,200.

The amount that will be deducted from the pool as proceeds when the disposal is made is:

£	

Test 2

Nitin, who prepares accounts to 30 September each year, had a balance on his main pool of £22,500 on 1 October 2013. In the year to 30 September 2014 he sold one asset and bought one asset as follows:

Addition (eligible for AIA) 1.5.14	£402,500
Disposal proceeds on sale on 1.8.14 (less than cost)	£7,800

The amount of capital allowances available for year ended 30 September 2014 is:

£	

Test 3

A company starts to trade on 1 July 2014, making up accounts to 31 December, and buys a car with CO_2 emission of 115g/km costing £18,000 on 15 July 2014. The company also buys energy-saving plant costing £5,000 on 1 September 2014.

The capital allowances available in the first period of account to 31 December 2014 are:

£	

Test 4

Abdul ceased trading on 31 December 2014 drawing up his final accounts for the year to 31 December 2014.

The following facts are relevant:

Main pool balance at 1.1.14	£12,500
Addition – 31.5.14	£20,000
Disposal proceeds (in total – proceeds not exceeding cost on any item) – 31.12.14	£18,300

Identify whether the following statement is True or False. Tick ONE box.

There is a balancing charge of £14,200 arising for the year to 31 December 2014.

	✓
True	
False	

Test 5

Raj, a sole trader who makes up accounts to 30 April each year, buys a Volvo estate car, with CO_2 emissions of 180g/km, for £30,000 on 31 March 2015. 60% of his usage of the car is for business purposes.

The capital allowance available to Raj in respect of the car for y/e 30 April 2015 is:

£	

chapter 4:
TAXING UNINCORPORATED BUSINESSES

---

chapter coverage 📖

Individuals must pay tax for each tax year. In this chapter we see what is meant by a tax year and we learn how to arrive at the trading profits to be taxed in each tax year.

The topics that we shall cover are:

✎   Basis periods

✎   Continuing businesses

✎   The start of trading

✎   Overlap profits

✎   The cessation of trading

INTRODUCTION

This chapter will concentrate on computing the figure to insert as **trading profit** in the income tax computation. Note that this only applies to unincorporated businesses. We will see how incorporated businesses (ie companies) bring the trading figure into the corporation tax computation, later in the Text.

In Chapter one we saw that 'trading profits' appear in the non-savings income column of a trader's income tax computation. The income tax computation is always completed for a period referred to as the **tax year, fiscal year, or year of assessment**.

The TAX YEAR, FISCAL YEAR or YEAR OF ASSESSMENT runs from 6 April in one year to 5 April in the next year. For example, 2014/15 runs from 6 April 2014 to 5 April 2015.

Chapters two and three dealt with the rules on how to work out taxable trading profits. Firstly we learnt how to adjust the accounting profit of a business in order to comply with tax legislation, and then how to calculate the capital allowances that are 'allowable' deductions from the trading profit.

However, as we have seen, all traders do not necessarily make up their accounts to coincide with a tax year. This chapter primarily looks at which profits fall into which tax year.

BASIS PERIODS

Traders can produce their business accounts to any date in the year they choose. However, as we have seen, income tax is charged for tax years. This means that a mechanism is needed to link the **taxable trading profits** (as adjusted for tax purposes and after the deduction of capital allowances) to a tax year. This mechanism is known as the **basis of assessment**, and the period whose profits are assessed in a tax year is called the BASIS PERIOD.

CONTINUING BUSINESSES

The basis of assessment for a continuing business is the **12 month period** of account **ending** in a tax year. The profits resulting from those accounts are taxed in that tax year. This is known as the CURRENT YEAR BASIS OF ASSESSMENT.

HOW IT WORKS

If a trader prepares accounts to 30 April each year, the profits of the year to 30 April 2014 will be taxed in 2014/15. This is because the year to 30 April 2014 ENDS in 2014/15 (ie between the dates 6 April 2014 and 5 April 2015).

Task 1

Talet, a dressmaker, has been in business for many years and prepares accounts to 30 September each year.

Identify her basis period for 2014/15. Tick ONE box.

	✓
1 October 2014 to 30 September 2015	
1 April 2014 to 31 March 2015	
1 October 2013 to 30 September 2014	
6 April 2014 to 5 April 2015	

THE START OF TRADING

On commencement of trade, the trader might not make up his first set of accounts for a 12 month period, therefore **special rules are needed to find the basis period in the first three tax years of a new business**. These rules always apply, even if the first set of accounts is for a 12 month period.

The first tax year

The tax year in which a trade starts is the first year in which profits will be taxed.

Identify the tax year that the date of commencement falls into.

HOW IT WORKS

If a trade starts on 15 May 2014, the first tax year in which profits are taxed is 2014/15. This is the tax year into which the date of commencement falls (ie 15 May 2014 falls between 6 April 2014 and 5 April 2015).

This rule ensures that profits are taxed right from the start of a business.

The basis period for the first tax year runs from the date the trade starts to the next 5 April (or to the date of cessation if the trade does not continue until the end of the tax year).

If accounts are not prepared to the end of the first tax year, you will need to time apportion taxable profits arising from one or more periods of account. For assessment purposes all time apportionment should be made on a monthly basis.

HOW IT WORKS

Sasha starts a trade on 1 December 2014. She prepares her first accounts for the ten months to 30 September 2015. The taxable profits arising as a result of these accounts are £60,000.

2014/15 is the tax year in which Sasha's trade starts, so the first year in which profits are taxed is 2014/15. The basis period for 2014/15 therefore, will run from 1 December 2014 to 5 April 2015. Taxable profits of £60,000 × 4/10 = £24,000 arise in this period and will be taxed in 2014/15.

The second tax year

Finding the basis period for the second tax year is tricky because there are three possibilities:

(a) If there is period of account that ends in the second tax year, but it is less than 12 months long, the basis period that must be used is the first 12 months of trading (ie increase the period to 12 months).

(b) If there is a period of account that ends in the second tax year, but is 12 months or longer, the basis period that must be used is the 12 months leading up to the end of that period of account (ie reduce the period to 12 months, if necessary).

(c) If there is no period of account that ends in the second tax year, because the first period of account is a very long one which does not end until a date in the third tax year, the basis period that must be used for the second tax year is the tax year itself (from 6 April to 5 April).

Some students find the following flowchart helpful in determining the basis period for the second tax year:

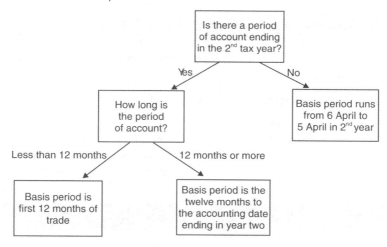

You can now use the flowchart to see if it helps you with the following examples:

HOW IT WORKS

Period of account ending in second tax year less than 12 months long

Janet starts trading on 1 July 2014. She prepares accounts for the ten months to 30 April 2015 and annually thereafter.

Janet's basis periods for the first two tax years of her business are:

Year	Basis period	
2014/15	1.7.14 – 5.4.15	(commencement to next 5 April)
2015/16	12 m to 30.06.15	(first 12 months of trade)

HOW IT WORKS

Period of account ending in second tax year 12 months or longer

John starts trading on 1 July 2014. He prepares accounts for the fifteen months to 30 September 2015.

John's basis periods for the first two tax years are:

Year	Basis period	
2014/15	1.7.14 – 5.4.15	(commencement to next 5 April)
2015/16	12 m to 30.9.15	(12 months to the accounting date ending in second tax year)

HOW IT WORKS

No period of account ending in second tax year

Abdul starts trading on 1 January 2014 and prepares accounts for the sixteen months to 30 April 2015.

Abdul's basis periods for the first two tax years are:

Year	Basis period	
2013/14	1.1.14 – 5.4.14	(commencement to next 5 April)
2014/15	6.4.14 – 5.4.15	(tax year)

Note that it was important to take care here and realise that the first tax year was 2013/14. This is because 1 January 2014 falls in 2013/14.

The third tax year

Finding the basis period in the third tax year is easier than the second tax year.

The basis period in the third tax year is always the 12 months to the end of the period of account ending in that year.

HOW IT WORKS

On 1 January 2014, Shamimma started trading. She prepares accounts to 31 December each year. What are the basis periods for the first three tax years of trading?

Solution

2013/14	1.1.14 – 5.4.14	(commencement to next 5 April)
2014/15	year to 31.12.14	(period of account ending in second tax year)
2015/16	year to 31.12.15	(12 month period ending in third tax year)

Now you can try a Task in which you must allocate taxable profits to the first three tax years. Remember that time apportionment for assessment purposes is done on a monthly basis.

Task 2

Kumar starts to trade on 1 June 2013, with the following results.

Period	Profit £
1.6.13 – 31.5.14	12,000
1.6.14 – 31.5.15	21,000

Using the proforma layout provided, show the taxable profits for each tax year from 2013/14 to 2015/16.

Tax year	Basis period	Taxable profits £

OVERLAP PROFITS

You may have noticed that the basis periods in the first three tax years of a new business may overlap with each other. This results in profits in the early years of a trade being taxed more than once.

Profits which have been taxed more than once are called OVERLAP PROFITS.

Some profits may be taxed twice because the basis period for the second tax year includes some or all of the period of trading in the first tax year or because the basis period for the third tax year overlaps with that for the second tax year.

HOW IT WORKS

Canning started a trade on 1 January 2013 and has the following results:

Period	Profit £
1.1.13 – 30.6.13	28,500
1.7.13 – 30.6.14	48,000
1.7.14 – 30.6.15	70,000

The taxable profits are as follows:

Year	Basis period	Working	Taxable profits £
2012/13	1.1.13 – 5.4.13	£28,500 × 3/6	14,250
2013/14	1.1.13 – 31.12.13	£28,500 + £48,000 × 6/12	52,500
2014/15	1.7.13 – 30.6.14		48,000
2015/16	1.7.14– 30.6.15		70,000

Overlap profits are:

	£
1.1.13 – 5.4.13	14,250
1.7.13 – 31.12.13	24,000
	38,250

Task 3

Harriet starts a trade on 1 March 2013, and has the following results.

Period	Profit £
1.3.13 – 30.6.14	32,000
1.7.14 – 30.6.15	36,800

(1) Using the proforma layout provided, show the taxable profits for the first four tax years

Tax year	Basis period	Taxable profits £

(2) The overlap profits are:

£ [ ]

THE CESSATION OF TRADING

You have seen the special basis period rules that apply in the first three tax years of a business. There are also special rules that apply in the last tax year that a business is carried on.

The final year of assessment is the tax year that the date of cessation falls into. **The basis period for this final tax year normally runs from the end of the basis period for the previous tax year to the date of cessation.**

Exceptionally, if a trade starts and ceases in the same tax year, the basis period for that year is the whole lifespan of the trade. If the final year is the second year, the basis period runs from 6 April at the start of the second year to the date of cessation.

Task 4

Malcolm has been trading for many years. His results for the last four periods of account before he ceased trading on 31 January 2015 are:

y/e 30.6.12	£12,000
y/e 30.6.13	£8,000
y/e 30.6.14	£6,000
p/e 31.1.15	£5,000

Using the proforma layout provided show the taxable profits for the years 2012/13 to 2014/15 inclusive before considering any overlap relief (see below).

Tax year	Basis period	Taxable profits £

When the trade ceases overlap profits are deducted from the final tax year's taxable profits. This means that over the life of a business, all of its total taxable profits, and no more, will have been taxed.

Task 5

Rex trades from 1 May 2010 to 31 January 2015, with the following results.

Period	Profit £
1.5.10 – 30.4.11	15,000
1.5.11 – 30.4.12	9,000
1.5.12 – 30.4.13	10,500
1.5.13 – 30.4.14	16,000
1.5.14 – 31.1.15	950
	51,450

Using the proforma layout provided show the taxable profits for all relevant tax years.

Tax year	Basis period	Taxable profits £
Total taxable trading profits		

Assessment focus

None of the information in this chapter is included within the 'Taxation Data' which you will be provided with in the live assessment.

The information included in this chapter typically will be tested in the following task:

Task 3 – Basis periods for sole traders and partnerships

Performance feedback

The feedback given below relates to students' performance on the AQ2010 version of the assessments. However, the points made by the assessor will be equally as valid for students sitting the assessment under AQ2013.

Task 1.3

'Assessment rules for sole traders and partnerships are covered in this task, and it is the second most poorly performed task in Section 1 for student performance. The vast majority of students only gain half, or less, of the available marks.

The issue seems not be the understanding of dates, but the computation of amounts. For instance, if a question asked for the dates applicable for the second year of trading, together with the amount taxable, the dates would be accurately shown, but with the wrong profit. It is a well-recognised fact that students struggle with working out numbers of months, but this issue is costing valuable marks.

It is recommended that students take their time over the computational aspects in these questions. Using fingers is fine in the exam, if it results in an accurate figure'.

CHAPTER OVERVIEW

- The profits of a 12 month period of account ending in a tax year are normally taxed in that tax year

- In the first tax year, the basis period runs from the date the business starts to the following 5 April

- There are three possibilities in the second tax year:

  - If a period of account of 12 months or more ends in the second tax year, the basis period for the second tax year is the 12 months to the end of that period of account

  - If a period of account of less than 12 months ends in the second tax year, the basis period for the second tax year is the first 12 months from the start of trading

  - If no period of account ends in the second tax year, the basis period for that year is 6 April to 5 April in the year

- The basis period for the third tax year is the 12 months to the end of the period of account ending in that year

- The basis period in the final tax year of a business runs from the end of the previous basis period to the date that the trade stops

- When a trade ceases overlap profits are deducted from the final tax year's taxable profits

Keywords

The **tax year**, **fiscal year** or **year of assessment** – is the year from 6 April in one year to 5 April in the next year

Basis period – is the period whose profits are taxed in a tax year

The **current year basis of assessment** – taxes the 12 month period of account ending in that tax year

Overlap profits – are the profits that are taxed more than once when a business starts

TEST YOUR LEARNING

Test 1

Oliver starts to trade on 1 May 2014. He makes his first set of accounts up to 31 December 2014 and annually thereafter.

Fill in the following table setting out the basis periods for the first three tax years and the overlap period of profits.

Tax year	Basis period
Overlap profits	

Test 2

Identify whether the following statement is True or False.

When the trade ceases overlap profits are deducted from the final tax year's taxable profits.

	✓
True	
False	

Test 3

Barlow stops trading on 31 December 2014 having been in business since January 2007. Previously he has always made accounts up to 31 May. Overlap profits on commencement were £10,000.

Results for the last few years (as adjusted for tax) are:

Period	Profits £
Period to 31.12.14	15,000
Year ended 31.5.14	25,000
Year ended 31.5.13	32,000
Year ended 31.5.12	18,000

Using the proforma layout provided, compute the taxable profits for the final three tax years of trading.

Tax year	Basis period	Taxable profits £

Test 4

Amarjat started trading on 1 February 2014. He prepared his first accounts to 30 June 2015. Taxable profits for this 17 month period were £34,000.

Show the taxable profits for 2013/14, 2014/15 and 2015/16.

Tax year	Basis period	Taxable profits £

His overlap profits are:

£	

Test 5

Susi started to trade on 1 December 2013. Her first accounts were prepared to 30 June 2014. Taxable profits for the first two periods of account were:

Period to 30 June 2014 £70,000

Year to 30 June 2015 £60,000

(1) **Her taxable profits for 2013/14 are:**

£	

(2) **Her taxable profits for 2014/15 are:**

£	

(3) **Her taxable profits for 2015/16 are:**

£	

(4) **Her overlap profits are:**

£	

chapter 5:
PARTNERSHIPS

chapter coverage 📖

You should recall that a partnership is a group of self employed individuals (partners) trading together. In this Chapter we see how to compute a partnership's taxable trading profits and how these profits are divided between and taxed on the individual partners. We look at situations where there is a change in the partnership profit sharing arrangements and where partners join or leave partnerships.

You may be asked to complete the tax return for a partnership.

The topics that we shall cover are:

✎ Computing taxable trading profits of partnerships

✎ Dividing taxable trading profits between partners

✎ The tax positions of individual partners

✎ Partnership investment income

✎ Partnership tax return

COMPUTING TAXABLE TRADING PROFITS OF PARTNERSHIPS

A PARTNERSHIP is a **group of self employed individuals** who are trading together.

A partnership prepares a statement of profit or loss in exactly the same way as a sole trader would. This statement of profit or loss is for the partnership business as a whole.

The profit for the year in the partnership statement of profit or loss must be adjusted for tax purposes in exactly the same way as you would adjust the profit for the year in the accounts of a sole trader. This means that you must add back disallowable items. You must deduct specifically deductible items that have not been deducted in the accounts (for example capital allowances) and also any income in the accounts that is not part of the taxable trading profit. Finally, add any amounts taxable as trading profits that have not been included in the accounts. For example, the market value of any goods taken for own use.

A particular point worth noting is that any partners' salaries or interest on capital deducted in the accounts must be added back when computing taxable trading profits of the partnership. These items are disallowable expenses because they are a form of drawings. They will be part of each partner's taxable trading profit as described below.

DIVIDING TAXABLE TRADING PROFITS BETWEEN PARTNERS

Once you have computed a partnership's taxable trading profit for a period of account, you must divide it between the partners concerned.

The partners may agree to share profits in any way they wish. The agreed division of profits will be set out in the partnership agreement and will always be stated for you in assessment tasks.

HOW IT WORKS

The Yellow partnership has tax adjusted profits of £40,000 for the year to 31 March 2015. The partners, Mr Blue and Mr Red, have agreed to share profits three quarters to Mr Blue and one quarter to Mr Red.

For the year to 31 March 2015, Mr Blue has taxable trading profits of £40,000 × ¾ = £30,000 andMr Red has taxable trading profits of £40,000 × ¼ = £10,000.

Note that Mr Blue and Mr Red would then allocate their individual trading profits to the appropriate tax year for income tax, as we saw in the last chapter.

Sometimes, rather than just divide profits between the partners in accordance with an agreed profit sharing ratio, the partners may agree that some or all of the partners should:

(a)   Be paid a 'salary' and/or
(b)   Be paid interest on the capital they contributed to the partnership.

In this case, your starting point in dividing a partnership's taxable profits between the partners should be to deal with any salary or interest on capital. Once you have done this you can divide the balance of any taxable trading profits between the partners in accordance with the profit sharing ratio.

HOW IT WORKS

Pearl and Ruby are in partnership. The partnership's taxable trading profits (as adjusted for tax purposes) for the year ended 31 March 2015 were £110,000. The partnership agreement provides for Pearl to be paid a salary of £20,000 per annum and for Ruby to be paid a salary of £30,000 per annum. Any remaining profits are divided between Pearl and Ruby in the ratio 2:1.

First allocate the partners' salaries and then divide the balance of the profit in accordance with the profit sharing ratio:

	Total £	Pearl £	Ruby £
Salary	50,000	20,000	30,000
Profit (£110,000 – £30,000 – £20,000) 2:1	60,000	40,000	20,000
	110,000	60,000	50,000

Pearl has taxable profits of £60,000 and Ruby has taxable profits of £50,000 for the year ended 31 March 2015.

Task 1

Roger and Muggles are in partnership. Tax adjusted trading profits for the year to 31 December 2014 were £210,000. The partnership agreement states that profits should be divided between Roger and Muggles in the ratio 4:1 after paying a salary of £30,000 per annum to each of the partners.

The taxable trading profit for Roger for the year to 31 December 2014 is:

£ [ ]

and the taxable trading profit for Muggles for the year to 31 December 2014 is:

£ [ ]

You should approach questions where the partnership agreement provides for interest on capital in exactly the same way. This means that you should allocate any interest on capital to the partners before dividing the balance of the profit in the agreed profit sharing ratio.

HOW IT WORKS

Sunita and Jim have been trading in partnership for several years. The partnership prepares accounts to 31 December each year and the taxable trading profits for the year to 31 December 2014 are £140,000. The partnership agreement provides for the following salaries, rates of interest on capital and share of remaining profits:

	Salary per annum £	Interest on capital %	Division of profit %
Sunita	45,000	3	50
Jim	25,000	3	50

The capital account balances of Sunita and Jim are £40,000 and £10,000 respectively.

The profits of the year to 31 December 2014 are allocated between the partners in the following way:

	Total £	Sunita £	Jim £
Salary	70,000	45,000	25,000
Interest on capital (40,000/ 10,000 × 3%)	1,500	1,200	300
Profits (£140,000 − 70,000 − 1,500) 50:50	68,500	34,250	34,250
Taxable profits	140,000	80,450	59,550

Task 2

James, Kieran and Jemima are in partnership. For the year to 31 December 2014 taxable trading profits were £270,000. They contributed capital of £20,000 each to the partnership. The partnership agreement provides for interest on capital of 5% to each party and salaries of £35,000 to be paid to Kieran and Jemima. James is not paid a salary. Remaining profits are divided between James, Kieran and Jemima in the ratio 3:1:1.

Using the proforma layout provided, show how these profits for the year to 31 December 2014 are allocated between the partners. Input 0 if your answer is zero.

	Total £	James £	Kieran £	Jemima £
Interest on capital				
Salaries				
Division of profits 3:1:1				
Taxable trading profits				

Change in the profit sharing agreement

Sometimes the agreed profit sharing arrangements may change during a period of account. If this happens, firstly you should time apportion the profits to before and after the change, and then divide them between the partners.

HOW IT WORKS

Jenny and Chris are in partnership. Taxable trading profits of the partnership for the year ended 31 March 2015 are £60,000. Until 30 September 2014 profits are shared equally. From 1 October 2014 Jenny and Chris agree that the profits should be shared in the ratio 2:1.

Show how the taxable trading profits of the year to 31 March 2015 are divided between Jenny and Chris.

Your first step should be to apportion the profits to the periods before and after the change in the profit sharing ratio:

1.4.14 – 30.9.14   6/12 × £60,000 = £30,000

1.10.14 – 31.3.15 6/12 × £60,000 = £30,000

Next divide these profits between the partners:

	Total £	Jenny £	Chris £
1.4.14 – 30.9.14 (1:1)	30,000	15,000	15,000
1.10.14 – 31.3.15 (2:1)	30,000	20,000	10,000
	60,000	35,000	25,000

For the year to 31 March 2015, Jenny's taxable trading profits are £35,000 and Chris' taxable trading profits are £25,000.

Task 3

Hansel and Greta are in partnership. The partnership accounts are prepared to 30 June each year. The taxable trading profits for the year ended 30 June 2014 were £80,000. Until 31 March 2014 Hansel and Greta shared profits equally. From 1 April 2014 they shared profits in the ratio 4:1.

(1)   Using the proforma layout provided, show how the profits are apportioned between the periods before and after the change in profit sharing ratio:

	£
Total profits	

(2) Using the proforma layout provided, calculate the taxable profits for each partner for the year to 30 June 2014.

	Total £	Hansel £	Greta £

A change in the rate at which salaries or interest are paid during a period of account has similar implications. You should time apportion the profits before and after the change and deal with each period separately. **Remember that the salaries and interest will need to be time apportioned too according to the agreements for each period.**

THE TAX POSITIONS OF INDIVIDUAL PARTNERS

Once you have allocated taxable profits for a period of account between partners, you must decide which tax year the profits are taxed in.

The current year basis of assessment applies to partnerships in the same way as it does to sole traders. For example, if a partnership prepares accounts to 30 June each year, the year to 30 June 2014 is the basis period for 2014/15 and a partner will be taxed on his share of the profits arising in the year ended 30 June 2014 in 2014/15.

Changes in partners

Sometimes the partners within a partnership change. **If a new partner joins a partnership, the special opening year rules** (that we saw in Chapter 4) **for sole traders apply to the new partner.** The existing partners continue to be taxed using the current year basis of assessment.

Similarly, **if a partner leaves a partnership, the closing year rules apply to that partner** as though he were a sole trader but the other partners continue to be taxed using the current year basis of assessment.

HOW IT WORKS: PARTNER JOINING A PARTNERSHIP

Francis and Caroline have been in partnership for many years making up accounts to 31 December each year. Profits were shared equally until 1 June 2012, when Charles joined the partnership. From 1 June 2012 profits were shared in the ratio 2:2:1.

Profits adjusted for tax purposes are as follows.

Period	Taxable profit
	£
1.1.12 – 31.12.12	48,000
1.1.13 – 31.12.13	18,000
1.1.14 – 31.12.14	24,000

Show the taxable profits for each partner for 2012/13 to 2014/15.

We must first share the profits between the partners.

	Total £	Francis £	Caroline £	Charles £
Year ended 31.12.12				
1.1.12 – 31.5.12 (5/12)				
Profits 50:50	20,000	10,000	10,000	
1.6.12 – 31.12.12 (7/12)				
Profits 2:2:1	28,000	11,200	11,200	5,600
Total	48,000	21,200	21,200	5,600
Year ended 31.12.13				
Profits 2:2:1	18,000	7,200	7,200	3,600
Total for y/e 31.12.13	18,000	7,200	7,200	3,600
Year ended 31.12.14				
Profits 2:2:1	24,000	9,600	9,600	4,800
Total for y/e 31.12.14	24,000	9,600	9,600	4,800

The next stage is to work out the basis periods and hence the taxable profits for the partners in each tax year. The most important thing to remember at this stage is to **deal with each of the partners separately**.

Francis and Caroline are taxed on the current year basis of assessment throughout.

Year	Basis period	Francis	Caroline
		£	£
2012/13	1.1.12 – 31.12.12	21,200	21,200
2013/14	1.1.13– 31.12.13	7,200	7,200
2014/15	1.1.14 – 31.12.14	9,600	9,600

Charles joins the partnership on 1 June 2012 which falls in tax year 2012/13 so the opening year rules apply to him from 2012/13.

Year	Basis period	Working	Taxable profits £
2012/13	1.6.12 – 5.4.13	£5,600 + 3/12 × £3,600	6,500
2013/14	1.1.13 – 31.12.13		3,600
2014/15	1.1.14 – 31.12.14		4,800

Charles has overlap profits of £900 (£3,600 x 3/12) to carry forward and relieve in the tax year in which he leaves the partnership.

HOW IT WORKS: PARTNER LEAVING A PARTNERSHIP

Dominic, Sebastian and India have traded in partnership sharing profits equally for many years. On 1 May 2014 India left the partnership. Profits continue to be shared equally. Accounts have always been prepared to 30 September and recent results have been:

	Profit £
Y/e 30.9.12	36,000
Y/e 30.9.13	81,000
Y/e 30.9.14	60,000

Each of the partners had overlap profits of £10,000 on commencement of the business. Show the taxable trading profits of each partner for 2012/13 to 2014/15.

Firstly allocate the profits of each period of account to the partners.

	Total £	Dominic £	Sebastian £	India £
Y/e 30.9.12	36,000	12,000	12,000	12,000
Y/e 30.9.13	81,000	27,000	27,000	27,000
Y/e 30.9.14				
1.10.13 – 30.4.14 (7/12)	35,000	11,667	11,667	11,666
1.5.14– 30.9.14 (5/12)	25,000	12,500	12,500	–
	60,000	24,167	24,167	11,666

Dominic and Sebastian are taxed on the continuing basis of assessment throughout:

	Dominic £	Sebastian £
2012/13 (y/e 30.9.12)	12,000	12,000
2013/14 (y/e 30.9.13)	27,000	27,000
2014/15 (y/e 30.9.14)	24,167	24,167

India is treated as ceasing to trade in 2014/15.

	£
2012/13 (y/e 30.9.12)	12,000
2013/14 (y/e 30.9.13)	27,000
2014/15 (p/e 30.4.14 less overlap profits)	
(£11,666 – £10,000)	1,666

Task 4

A partnership makes profits as follows.

	£
Year ended 31 October 2013	34,200
Year ended 31 October 2014	45,600

A partner joins on 1 June 2013 and is entitled to 30% of the profits.

His taxable profits for 2013/14 are:

£ ☐

His overlap profits carried forward are:

£ ☐

His taxable profits for 2014/15 are:

£ ☐

Task 5

X, Y and Z have traded in partnership for many years sharing profits equally. On 1 July 2013 X retired. Y and Z continue trading, sharing profits in the ratio 3:2.

There were no unrelieved overlap profits on commencement of the business.

The profits of the partnership as adjusted for tax purposes are as follows.

	Profit £
Year to 31 March 2013	24,000
Year to 31 March 2014	14,000
Year to 31 March 2015	48,000

(1) Using the proforma layout provided, show the division of partnership profits in the three years to 31 March 2015. Input 0 if your answer is zero.

	Total £	X £	Y £	Z £
Year ended 31/3/2013				
Year ended 31/3/2014				
Year ended 31/3/2015				

(2) Using the information from part (1) complete the following table showing the amounts taxable on each partner in the relevant tax years. Input 0 if your answer is zero.

	X	Y	Z

PARTNERSHIP INVESTMENT INCOME

A partnership may also have investment income such as interest on a bank account.

Partnership investment income is shared between partners in a similar way to trading income using the profit sharing ratios applicable to the period in which the investment income is received.

PARTNERSHIP TAX RETURN

In your assessment you may be asked to complete the partnership summary of the partnership tax return. A copy of this page is available at the end of this chapter. Have a good look at the extract. You will be able to practise completing this return in the Business Tax Question Bank.

Assessment focus

AAT sample assessments in the past have included a figure for 'CIS contractor's tax deducted'. This relates to tax that has been deducted under the 'Construction Industry Scheme' which is not a topic which you need to understand for the Business Tax assessment.

You do not need to understand the Construction Industry Scheme to complete this Task. Instead, this Task is only expecting you to insert the tax figure (given in the Task) into the relevant box of the partnership tax return, which is Box 24. It would be wise to familiarise yourself with this and the other boxes in the return, as the assessor has confirmed 'students are expected to read the question and input figures corresponding to the question'.

Assessment focus

None of the information in this chapter is included within the 'Taxation Data' which you will be provided with in the live assessment.

The information included in this chapter typically will be tested in the following task:

Task 3– Split of partnership profits for new, continuing and leaving partners. Basis periods for sole traders and partnerships

Performance feedback

The feedback given below relates to students' performance on the AQ2010 version of the assessments. However, the points made by the assessor will be equally as valid for students sitting the assessment under AQ2013.

Task 1.3 (AQ2010)

See performance feedback in Chapter 4

Task 1.5 (AQ2010)

'This task covers allocation of profits within a partnership and is easily the best answered task in Section 1. This could be due to students applying their knowledge from previous AAT assessments.

The only recurring issue is with students failing to read numbers of months accurately.

For example, if a partnership has a 31 October year end, and the salary of one partner started on 1 April, students either fail to time apportion the annual salary, or they use six months instead of seven.

CHAPTER OVERVIEW

- A partnership is a group of self employed individuals trading together

- Calculate tax adjusted profits for a partnership in the same way as you would calculate the tax adjusted profits of a sole trader

- Divide the tax adjusted profits of a period of account between the partners in accordance with their profit sharing arrangements during the period of account

- If profit sharing arrangements change during a period of account, time apportion profits to the periods before and after the change before allocating them to partners

- Once you have found a partner's profit for a period of account you can consider which tax year that profit is taxed in. A continuing partner in a continuing business is taxed using the current year basis of assessment

- The opening year rules apply to a partner joining the partnership. The closing year rules apply to a partner leaving the partnership

Keywords

Partnership – is a group of self employed individuals trading together

TEST YOUR LEARNING

Test 1

The adjusted profit of a partnership is divided between the partners in accordance with the profit sharing agreement in existence during what period? Tick ONE box

	✓
The calendar year	
The tax year	
The period of account concerned	
The period agreed by the partners	

Test 2

Dave and Joe are in partnership together and make a profit of £18,000 for the year to 31 December 2014. Up to 30 September 2014 they share profits and losses equally but thereafter they share 3:2.

Dave's taxable profits for 2014/15 are:

£

and Joe's taxable profits for 2014/15 are:

£

Test 3

Holly and Jasmine are in partnership sharing profits equally after paying a salary of £5,000 to Holly and a salary of £80,000 to Jasmine. Taxable profits for the year to 31 March 2015 were £200,000.

Using the proforma layout provided, show the taxable profits of each of the partners for the year.

	Total £	Holly £	Jasmine £
Salary			
Division of profits			

Test 4

Barry and Steve have been in partnership for many years. Profits are shared three-quarters to Barry and one-quarter to Steve. For the year ended 31 March 2014, the partnership made a profit of £60,000 and for the year ended 31 March 2015 the profit was £80,000.

The profit taxable on Steve for 2014/15 is:

	✓
£60,000	
£15,000	
£45,000	
£20,000	

Tick ONE box

Test 5

Abdul and Ghita have been in partnership for many years. On 1 September 2014, Sase joins the partnership and profits are shared 2:2:1. For the year to 31 August 2015, the partnership makes a profit of £120,000.

The profits assessable on Sase in 2014/15 are:

£ _____

The profits assessable on Sase in 2015/16 are:

£ _____

The overlap profits arising for Sase are:

£ _____

BPP
LEARNING MEDIA

Test 6

William, Ann and John have been in partnership for many years sharing profits equally. Accounts have always been prepared to 31 October each year. All partners had overlap profits of £5,000 on commencement. On 31 December 2014 William left the partnership. Profits continued to be shared equally. Recent results were:

	£
Y/e 31 October 2013	21,000
Y/e 31 October 2014	33,000
Y/e 31 October 2015	36,000

(1) **Using the proforma layout provided, show how the profits of each period will be divided between the partners.**

	Total £	William £	Ann £	John £
Y/e 31.10.13				
Y/e 31.10.14				
Y/e 31.10.15				

(2) **Using the proforma layout provided, show the taxable profits for each partner for 2013/14 to 2015/16.**

	William £	Ann £	John £

EXTRACT FROM PARTNERSHIP TAX RETURN

PARTNERSHIP STATEMENT (SHORT) *for the year ended 5 April 2015*

Please read these instructions before completing the Statement

Use these pages to allocate partnership income if the only income for the relevant return period was trading and professional income or taxed interest and alternative finance receipts from banks and building societies. Otherwise you must download or ask the SA Orderline for the *Partnership Statement (Full)* pages to record details of the allocation of all the partnership income. Go to hmrc.gov.uk/selfassessmentforms

Step 1 Fill in boxes 1 to 29 and boxes A and B as appropriate. Get the figures you need from the relevant boxes in the Partnership Tax Return. Complete a separate Statement for each accounting period covered by this Partnership Tax Return and for each trade or profession carried on by the partnership.

Step 2 Then allocate the amounts in boxes 11 to 29 attributable to each partner using the allocation columns on this page and page 7, read the Partnership Tax Return Guide, go to hmrc.gov.uk/selfassessmentforms If the partnership has more than three partners, please photocopy page 7.

Step 3 Each partner will need a copy of their allocation of income to fill in their personal tax return.

PARTNERSHIP INFORMATION

If the partnership business includes a trade or profession, enter here the accounting period for which appropriate items in this statement are returned.

Start **1** / /

End **2** / /

Nature of trade **3**

MIXED PARTNERSHIPS

Tick here if this Statement is drawn up using Corporation Tax rules **4**

Tick here if this Statement is drawn up using tax rules for non-residents **5**

Individual partner details

6 Name of partner

Address

Postcode

Date appointed as a partner (if during 2013–14 or 2014–15) **7** / /

Partner's Unique Taxpayer Reference (UTR) **8**

Date ceased to be a partner (if during 2013–14 or 2014–15) **9** / /

Partner's National Insurance number **10**

Partnership's profits, losses, income, tax credits, etc.

Tick this box if the items entered in the box had foreign tax taken off

Partner's share of profits, losses, income, tax credits, etc.

Copy figures in boxes 11 to 29 to boxes in the individual's Partnership (short) pages as shown below

- **for an accounting period ended in 2014–15** ▼

from box 3.83 Profit from a trade or profession **A**	**11** £	Profit **11** £	*Copy this figure to box 8*
from box 3.82 Adjustment on change of basis	**11A** £	**11A** £	*Copy this figure to box 10*
from box 3.84 Loss from a trade or profession **B**	**12** £	Loss **12** £	*Copy this figure to box 8*
from box 10.4 Business Premises Renovation Allowance	**12A** £	**12A** £	*Copy this figure to box 15*

- **for the period 6 April 2014 to 5 April 2015***

from box 7.9A UK taxed interest and taxed alternative finance receipts	**22** £	**22** £	*Copy this figure to box 28*
from box 3.97 CIS deductions made by contractors on account of tax	**24** £	**24** £	*Copy this figure to box 30*
from box 3.98 Other tax taken off trading income	**24A** £	**24A** £	*Copy this figure to box 31*
from box 7.8A Income Tax taken off	**25** £	**25** £	*Copy this figure to box 29*
from box 3.117 Partnership charges	**29** £	**29** £	*Copy this figure to box 4, 'Other tax reliefs' section on page Ai 2 in your personal tax return*

* If you are a 'CT Partnership' see the Partnership Tax Return Guide

SA800 2015 PARTNERSHIP TAX RETURN: PAGE 6

chapter 6:
COMPUTING TAXABLE TOTAL PROFITS

chapter coverage 📖

In this chapter we move on to corporation tax and see how to compute a company's taxable total profits for corporation tax. We also see that taxable total profits must be computed for accounting periods.

It is important that you can differentiate between the rules for individuals (and partnerships) and those for companies.

The topics that we shall cover are:

✍ Taxable total profits

✍ Long periods of account

TAXABLE TOTAL PROFITS

To arrive at the **profits on which a company must pay tax** you need to

- Aggregate the company's various sources of income and chargeable gains together

- Deduct the amount of any 'qualifying charitable donations' (Gift Aid donation) paid

The resulting figure is known as the company's TAXABLE TOTAL PROFITS. The computation is shown in the following proforma:

	£
Trading profits (as adjusted for tax)	X
Interest	X
Property business profits	X
Other income	X
Chargeable gains	X
Total profits	X
Less qualifying charitable donations paid	(X)
Taxable total profits	**X**

Dividends received from other companies are usually exempt from corporation tax and so not included in taxable total profits. You will not be expected to deal with non exempt UK dividends in your assessment.

We will now look at each of the items in the above proforma in turn.

Trading profits

The trading profits of a company are, broadly, computed in the same way that the trading profits of a sole trader are computed. You should, therefore, take the **profit for the year in the company's accounts and adjust it for tax purposes** in the same way as you would adjust a sole trader's accounting profit. We looked at adjustment of profit earlier in this Text.

As a reminder, two important differences are:

- There is never any private use adjustments for a company when either adjusting the accounting profit or calculating capital allowances.

- Companies deal with a long period of account (accounts that have been made up for more than 12 months) in a different way to individuals or partnerships.

We will look at long periods of account for companies below.

Task 1

N Ltd, a trading company, makes up its accounts to 31 March each year. In the year to 31 March 2015, the statement of profit or loss showed the following:

	£
Gross profit (note)	514,000
General expenses (all allowable)	(85,000)
Profit for the year	429,000

Note. Gross profit includes property business income of £4,000.

The company had a main pool with a value of £21,500 as at 1 April 2014. On 1 December 2014, the company bought a car with CO_2 emissions of 120g/km for £11,000. The car was used by a director of the company. It was agreed that 20% of the use of the car was private use by the director.

(1) Using the proforma layout provided, calculate the capital allowances available for the year to 31 March 2015.

	Main pool £	Allowances £
B/f		
Addition		
WDA		
C/f		

(2) Using the proforma layout provided, calculate the trading profits for the year to 31 March 2015.

	£
Profit for the year	429,000
Trading profits	

(3) Using the pro forma layout provided, calculate the taxable total profits for the year to 31 March 2015.

	£

Interest received

Companies receive NON-TRADING INTEREST **gross from banks and building societies** (ie no tax is deducted in advance from the amount received). Interest received from other companies (this includes debenture interest) is also received **gross**.

Interest paid

Companies may also PAY INTEREST for example on loans taken out by the company, including the issue of loan stock or debenture stock.

If the loan is for a **trading purpose** (eg to buy plant and machinery for use in the company's trade), **the interest is deductible when computing the company's trading income.** This means that if it is showing as an expense in the statement of profit or loss, NO adjustment is needed.

If the loan is for a **non-trading purpose** (eg to buy investments such as shares or properties to rent out), the interest is **deductible from interest received** (eg from a bank or building society) **to give a net 'interest' figure to be used in computing taxable total profits.** In some cases, there may be a deficit of non-trading interest paid over non-trading interest received, but the treatment of such a deficit is not in your syllabus.

Other costs of raising loan finance, such as fees, are dealt with in the same way as interest paid.

Property business income

A company with property business income must **pool the rents and expenses on all of its properties, to give a single profit or loss**. Property business income is taxed on an **accruals basis**.

You will not be expected to calculate property business income in your Business Tax assessment. However, you may be given a profit figure and be required to include it within the corporation tax computation as appropriate.

Chargeable gains

Companies do not pay capital gains tax. Instead their **net chargeable gains** (current period gains less current period and brought forward capital losses) **are brought into the computation of taxable total profits.**

Capital Gains Tax (for individuals) and chargeable gains for companies are dealt with later in this Text.

Qualifying charitable donations

Qualifying charitable donations are charitable gifts on which tax relief is given, however they cannot be deducted as a trading expense.

For companies, qualifying charitable donations paid are deducted in computing taxable total profits as shown in the proforma above. They have to be actually paid, not just accrued in the accounting period.

If a qualifying charitable donation has been deducted in computing the accounts profit, the amount deducted must be added back in computing taxable **trading** profits (adjustment of profits), but can then be deducted when computing taxable total profits.

Income received/paid net of tax

Companies receive patent royalties from individuals net of 20% income tax. This means that the individual withholds 20% tax and pays it over to HMRC on the company's behalf.

Income received net of tax is included within the corporation tax computation at its gross equivalent. For example £8,000 of patent royalties received net of tax would need to be grossed up by multiplying by 100/80 to include £10,000 within either trading profits or other income.

Patent royalties and interest, paid by a company to individuals are paid net of 20% income tax which the company pays over to HMRC. It is the gross amount that is deducted in the corporation tax computation, either from trading profits or from interest or other income as described above.

Payments of royalties and interest by a company to a company are made gross and so there are no income tax implications.

HOW IT WORKS

ST Ltd draws up accounts for the year ended 31 March 2015 which show the following results:

		£	£
Gross profit on trading			180,000
Dividends received from other companies			7,900
Bank interest received			222
Profit on sale of investments			20,000
Less	Trade expenses (all allowable)	83,400	
	Bank interest payable (overdraft)	200	
	Debenture interest payable (gross)	3,200	
	Qualifying charitable donation	100	
	Depreciation charge	9,022	(95,922)
Profit before taxation			112,200

Notes

1   The capital allowances for the accounting period total £5,500.

2   The debentures were issued on 1 August 2014 to raise working capital. The £3,200 charged in the accounts represents six months interest (£2,400) paid and two months accrued.

3   The profit on the sale of investments resulted in a chargeable gain of £13,867.

The calculation of the company's taxable total profits is as follows:

		£	£
Profit for the year per accounts			112,200
Less	Dividends received	7,900	
	Profit on investments	20,000	
	Interest received	222	
			(28,122)
			84,078
Add	Qualifying charitable donation	100	
	Depreciation charge	9,022	
			9,122
			93,200
Less	capital allowances		(5,500)
Trading profits			87,700
Interest received			222
Chargeable gain			13,867
			101,789
Less	qualifying charitable donation		(100)
Taxable total profits			101,689

Note. The dividends received from other companies are not included within taxable total profits.

Assessment focus

The Assessor has commented that students struggle to differentiate between trading profits and taxable total profits. Review the above and make sure you are happy with this.

Task 2

A company had the following results in the year ended 31 March 2015.

	£
Trading profits	85,000
Bank deposit interest income	6,000
Building society interest income	1,500
Dividends received	3,200
Chargeable gains	2,950
Qualifying charitable donation	15,200

The company's taxable total profits are:

£ [   ]

LONG PERIODS OF ACCOUNT

A PERIOD OF ACCOUNT is the period for which a company prepares its accounts.

An ACCOUNTING PERIOD is the period for which corporation tax is charged.

A company's accounting period is often the same as its period of account. However, **an accounting period cannot be longer than twelve months.** This means that **if a period of account exceeds 12 months, it must be divided into two accounting periods of**:

- The first 12 months
- The remaining balance of months

It is necessary to prepare separate computations of taxable total profits for each accounting period.

The following rules are applied in apportioning income, gains and qualifying charitable donations between accounting periods:

(a) **Trading income** (before deducting capital allowances) is apportioned on a **time basis**.

(b) **Capital allowances** and balancing charges are **calculated separately** for each accounting period.

(c) **Property business income** is apportioned on a **time basis** as applies for trading income.

(d) **Interest income** on non-trading loans is allocated to the **period in which it accrues**.

(e) Other income is apportioned on a time basis.

(f) **Chargeable gains** are allocated to the accounting **period in which the disposal takes place**.

(g) **Qualifying charitable donations** are allocated to the accounting **period in which they are paid**.

The apportionment rules are illustrated in the following example.

HOW IT WORKS

Beta Ltd makes up its accounts for a 15 month period ended 31 March 2015. Trading income is £150,000 for the 15 month period.

The brought forward balance on the main pool for capital allowances on 1 January 2014 was £32,000. The only capital expenditure that took place during this period was in February 2015 being the purchase of machinery for £15,000.

Bank deposit interest of £672 was received on 31 March 2014 and £1,402 on 31 March 2015. The amounts accrued at 1 January 2014 and 1 January 2015 were £412 and £950 respectively.

The company made a qualifying charitable donation payment of £3,630 on 14 March 2014.

Disposals of investments realised a chargeable gain of £5,300 on 14 March 2014 and a chargeable gain of £807 on 14 March 2015.

The company's taxable total profits are as follows:

	Note	AP 1.1.14 – 31.12.14 £	AP 1.1.15 – 31.3.15 £
Trading income (12/15 : 3/15)	1	120,000	30,000
Less capital allowances	W	(5,760)	(16,181)
Trading profits		114,240	13,819
Interest	W	1,210	452
Chargeable gains	2	5,300	807
Less qualifying charitable donation	3	(3,630)	–
Taxable total profits		117,120	15,078

Notes

1   Trading income is time apportioned.

2   Chargeable gains are allocated to the period in which the relevant disposal takes place.

3 Qualifying charitable donations are allocated to the period in which they are paid.

Workings

Capital allowances are calculated separately for each accounting period

	AIA £	Main pool £	Allowances £
12 m to 31 December 2014			
B/f		32,000	
WDA @ 18%		(5,760)	5,760
C/f		26,240	
3m to 31 March 2015			
AIA acquisition			
Machinery	15,000		
AIA (Max £500,000 × 3/12)	(15,000)		15,000
	0		
WDA @ 18% x 3/12		(1,181)	1,181
C/f		25,059	
			16,181

Interest income is allocated to the period in which it accrued as follows:

	12m to 31.12.14 £	3m to 31.3.15 £
Bank interest received	672	1,402
Less opening accrual	(412)	(950)
Add closing accrual	950	–
Amount accrued	1,210	452

Task 3

X Ltd makes up a 15 month set of accounts to 30 June 2015 with the following results.

	£
Trading profits	300,000
Interest 15 months @ £500 accruing per month	7,500
Chargeable gain (1 May 2014) disposal	250,000
Less qualifying charitable donation (paid 31.12.14)	(50,000)
	507,500

Using the proforma layout provided, calculate the taxable total profits for each of the accounting periods based on the above accounts. Input 0 if the answer is zero.

	.... ended......	.... ended......
	£	£

Assessment focus

In the live assessment you will be provided with 'Taxation Data' that can be accessed through pop up windows. The content of these taxation data tables has been reproduced at the front of this Text. Make sure you familiarise yourself with the content and practise referring to it as you work through this Text.

The information included in this chapter typically will be tested in the following task:

Task 4 – Taxable total profits and corporation tax payable

Performance feedback

The feedback given below relates to students' performance on the AQ2010 version of the assessments. However, the points made by the assessor will be equally as valid for students sitting the assessment under AQ2013.

Feedback on both Task 1.2 (AQ2010) and Task 1.7 (AQ2010) have been given within Chapters two and three respectively.

Task 1.6 (AQ2010)

'This is a reasonably well answered task in the main, but there are some recurring issues.

Students seem to struggle to understand the distinction between trading profits and taxable profit. Although the core text books cover this distinction clearly, students treat trading profits as taxable profits, and vice versa. Careful and thorough coverage of this topic is needed.

Another recurring error is the handling of long periods of account for limited companies. I have examples where students will split an 18 month period into 6/12 months rather than 12/6. This is a frequently assessed area and so must be studied with due care.'

CHAPTER OVERVIEW

- Adjustment of profit for companies is similar to that for individuals but there is no private use adjustment

- To compute taxable total profits aggregate all sources of income and chargeable gains. Deduct qualifying charitable donations

- Patent royalties and interest are received/paid to individuals net of 20% tax. Include the gross amounts in the computation of taxable total profits

- An accounting period cannot exceed 12 months in length

- A long period of account must be split into two accounting periods: a period of 12 months and then a period covering the balance of the period of account

Keywords

Taxable total profits – The profits on which a company must pay corporation tax

Period of account – The period for which a company prepares its accounts

Accounting period – The period for which corporation tax is charged

Qualifying charitable donations – Charitable gifts on which tax relief is given

TEST YOUR LEARNING

Test 1

Indicate whether the following statements are true or false.

Type of income	True	False
A company with a nine month period of account will calculate capital allowances for nine months and deduct them from adjusted trading profits		
A company with an eighteen month period of account will calculate capital allowances for eighteen months and deduct them from adjusted trading profits, and then prorate the answer between the appropriate accounting periods		
A company with an eighteen month period of account will calculate capital allowances for the first twelve months then capital allowances for the remaining six months and deduct them from the relevant prorated trading profits allocated to each accounting period		
Dividends are not included in the taxable total profits. They are taxed separately		

Test 2

A company has accrued interest payable of £4,000 (gross) for the year ended 31 March 2015.

The interest payable was paid on a loan taken out to buy some machinery for use in the company's trade.

Identify how will this be treated in the corporation tax computation. Tick ONE box

	✓
Added to trading income	
Added to net non-trading interest	
Deducted from trading income	
Deducted from net non-trading interest	

Test 3

On 30 June 2014, Edelweiss Ltd makes a donation to Help the Aged of £385. The donation is a qualifying charitable donation. **The amount of deduction available in respect of the charitable donation when calculating taxable total profits is:**

£	

Test 4

X Ltd had been making up accounts to 31 May for several years. Early in 2014 the directors decided to make accounts to 31 August 2014 (instead of 31 May 2014) and annually thereafter to 31 August.

Tick the box which correctly shows the two chargeable accounting periods for CT purposes for X Ltd.

	✓
1 June 2013 – 31 March 2014 and 1 April 2014 – 31 August 2014	
1 June 2013 – 31 May 2014 and 1 June 2014– 31 August 2014	
1 June 2013 – 31 December 2013 and 1 January 2014 – 31 August 2014	
1 June 2013 – 31 August 2013 and 1 September 2013 – 31 August 2014	

Test 5

C Ltd prepares accounts for the 16 months to 30 April 2015. The results are as follows:

	£
Trading profits	320,000
Bank interest received (accrued evenly over period)	1,600
Chargeable gain (made 1.1.15)	20,000
Qualifying charitable donation (paid 31.12.14)	15,000

Using the proforma layout provided, calculate the taxable total profits for the accounting periods based on the above results. Input 0 if your answer is zero.

	....ended....	....ended....
	£	£
Trading profits		
Interest		
Chargeable gain		
Qualifying charitable donation		
Taxable total profits		

chapter 7:
COMPUTING CORPORATION TAX PAYABLE

---

chapter coverage 📖

In this chapter we see how to compute the corporation tax that a company must pay on its taxable total profits. We start by looking at single companies with 12 month accounting periods. We then consider the effect of short accounting periods and the effect of a company being associated with other companies. You are also introduced to the page of the corporation tax return that you may have to complete in your assessment.

The topics that we shall cover are:

✎ Determining augmented profits

✎ Computing the corporation tax liability

✎ Short accounting periods

✎ Associated companies

✎ Company tax return form

INTRODUCTION

We have seen that sole traders, and partners within a partnership, pay income tax on their trading profits. We will now see now that companies pay corporation tax on their trading profits.

Having worked out the taxable total profits in the previous chapter, this chapter will look at how to calculate the corporation tax payable.

A company will pay corporation tax on its **taxable total profits** figure, however **'augmented profits'** will first need to be computed in order to decide the correct rate of tax to apply to the taxable total profits. It is important that you calculate the corporation tax on the taxable total profits figure and not the augmented profits.

DETERMINING AUGMENTED PROFITS

Corporation tax rates are fixed for financial years. A FINANCIAL YEAR runs from 1 April to the following 31 March and is identified by the calendar year in which it begins.

For example, the year ended 31 March 2015 is the Financial Year 2014 (FY 2014) as it begins on 1 April 2014. This should not be confused with a tax year for an individual, that runs from 6 April to the following 5 April.

The corporation tax rate for any particular Financial Year depends on the level of a company's AUGMENTED PROFITS. **Augmented profits are taxable total profits plus the grossed-up amount of dividends received from other companies.** The grossed-up amount of a dividend received is the dividend received grossed up by multiplying by 100/90. This is sometimes referred to as 'Franked Investment Income' (FII). The exception to this is dividends received from associated companies (see later in this chapter) that are not taken into account in a calculation of augmented profits.

HOW IT WORKS

A company had taxable total profits of £400,000 in the year ended 31 March 2015. In this year it received dividends of £9,000.

Augmented profits are:

	£
Taxable total profits	400,000
Dividend (£9,000 × 100/90)	10,000
Augmented profits	410,000

Task 1

A company had taxable total profits of £60,000 and dividends received of £4,500 in the year to 31 December 2014. The company's augmented profits for the year were:

£ [   ]

COMPUTING THE CORPORATION TAX LIABILITY

In this section we look at how to compute corporation tax for a twelve month accounting period where the company does not have associated companies. We will look at other situations later in this chapter.

To work out the CT rate that applies, augmented profits have to be compared with various limits. These limits will be available to you in the taxation data tables throughout the live assessment. Remember that corporation tax is always charged on the taxable total profits of a company.

The main rate of corporation tax

The MAIN RATE of corporation tax (CT) for Financial Year 2014 (FY2014) is 21%.

If a company's augmented profits exceed the upper limit for Financial Year 2014, the **main rate of corporation tax is charged** for the year. For the Financial Year 2014, the upper limit is £1,500,000.

HOW IT WORKS

A Ltd had the following results in the year to 31 March 2015:

Taxable total profits £1,450,000
Dividend received £90,000

Augmented profits for the year are £1,450,000 + (£90,000 × 100/90) = £1,550,000

As augmented profits are above the upper limit, the main rate of corporation tax applies.

Corporation tax due is £1,450,000 × 21% = £304,500

Note that although augmented profits are used to determine the rate of corporation tax, the rate is then applied only to taxable total profits.

Task 2

For the year to 31 March 2015, M Ltd had the following results:

	£
Taxable total profits	2,100,000
Dividend received	45,000

M Ltd's corporation tax liability for the year is:

£ [   ]

Marginal relief

Marginal relief applies where the augmented profits of an accounting period are between the lower and upper limits. For Financial Year 2014 these limits are £300,000 and £1,500,000.

To calculate corporation tax:

- First calculate the corporation tax at the main rate on taxable total profits
- Then deduct marginal relief using the formula:

$(U – A) \times N/A \times$ standard fraction

where   U   =   upper limit (currently £1,500,000)
             A   =   augmented profits
             N   =   taxable total profits

The standard fraction is 1/400 for FY 2014.

The marginal relief formula and the standard fraction will be available to you in the taxation data tables throughout the live assessment.

HOW IT WORKS

B Ltd has the following results for the year ended 31 March 2015:

	£
Taxable total profits	280,000
Dividend received 1 December 2014	45,000

First, calculate augmented profits to determine the rate of corporation tax:

	£
Taxable total profits	280,000
Dividends received (45,000 x 100/90)	50,000
Augmented profits	330,000

As augmented profits are between the lower and upper limits, marginal relief applies:

	£
Taxable total profits £280,000 @ 21%	58,800
Less 1/400 £(1,500,000 – 330,000) × $\dfrac{280,000}{330,000}$	(2,482)
Corporation tax payable	56,318

Task 3

For the year to 31 March 2015, M Ltd, has the following results:

	£
Trading profits	220,000
Dividend received	90,000

(1) Using the proforma layout provided, calculate the augmented profits of M Ltd for the year to 31 March 2015.

	£
Taxable total profits	
Dividends	
Augmented profits	

(2) Using the proforma layout provided, calculate the corporation tax liability of M Ltd for the year to 31 March 2015.

	£

Small profits rate (SPR)

The SPR of corporation tax (20% for FY 2014) applies to the taxable total profits of companies whose augmented profits are below the lower limit. For FY 2014 this limit is £300,000.

HOW IT WORKS

X Ltd had the following results for the year ended 31 March 2015:

	£
Taxable total profits	100,000
Dividend received	18,000

First calculate augmented profits:

	£
Taxable total profits	100,000
Dividend received (18,000 × 100/90)	20,000
Augmented profits	120,000

As augmented profits are below £300,000, the small profits rate of tax is applied to taxable total profits.

CT payable 20% × £100,000 = __£20,000__

Task 4

BD Ltd had the following results for the year to 31 March 2015:

Taxable total profits = £60,000

No dividends were received in the year.

The corporation tax liability for the year is:

£ [   ]

Periods straddling FY13 and FY14

The main rate of CT for FY 2013 is 23%.

There is no change to the SPR of 20% between FY13 and FY14, and there is no change to the limits of £300,000 and £1,500,000.

However, as there is a change in the main rate of corporation tax and the marginal relief standard fraction between these two Financial Years, they will need to be dealt with separately when calculating the CT liability of a large company (one with augmented profits above the upper limit) and a marginal

BPP
LEARNING MEDIA

company (one with augmented profits between the lower and upper limits). The standard fraction used in the marginal relief formula is 3/400 for FY 2013.

HOW IT WORKS

Claude Ltd makes up accounts to 30 September each year. For the year ended 30 September 2014 the company had taxable total profits of £1,800,000 and received dividends of £216,000.

Step 1   Identify which rate of CT to apply.

Work out the augmented profits to decide whether the small profits rate, marginal relief or the main rate should apply.

Augmented profits are £1,800,000 + £216,000 × 100/90 = £2,040,000

This means the main rate of CT applies.

Step 2   Determine the number of months that fall into FY13 and the number of months that fall into FY14 and apportion the taxable total profits accordingly.

With the year ended 30 September 2014, six months of the accounting period fall in FY13 (1 October 2013 to 31 March 2014) and six months fall into FY14 (1 April 2014 to 30 September 2014).

Step 3   Apply the correct rate of corporation tax to the separate apportioned taxable total profits for the corresponding FY.

Tax on taxable total profits (FY13)

£1,800,000 × 23% × **6/12** = £207,000

Tax on taxable total profits (FY14)

£1,800,000 × 21% × **6/12** = £189,000

Therefore total CT liability for year ended 30 September 2014 is £396,000.

HOW IT WORKS

Augustus Ltd makes up accounts to 30 June each year. For the year ended 30 June 2014 the company had taxable total profits of £550,000 and received dividends of £90,000.

Step 1   Identify which rate of CT to apply.

Augmented profits are £550,000 + £90,000 × 100/90 = £650,000

This means the marginal relief applies.

Step 2   Determine the number of months that fall into FY13 and the number of months that fall into FY14 and apportion the taxable total profits accordingly.

With the year ended 30 June 2014, nine months of the accounting period fall in FY13 (1 July 2013 to 31 March 2014) and three months fall into FY14 (1 April 2014 to 30 June 2014).

Step 3   Apply the correct rate of corporation tax to the separate apportioned taxable total profits for the corresponding FY.

Tax on taxable total profits (FY13)

£550,000 × 23% × **9/12** = £94,875

Less 3/400 £(1,500,000 − 650,000) × 550/650 × **9/12** =(4,046)

Tax on taxable total profits (FY14)

£550,000 × 21% × **3/12** = £28,875

Less 1/400 £(1,500,000 − 650,000) x 550/650 × **3/12** =(450)

Therefore total CT liability for year ended 30 June 2014 is £119,254

Note: There is no need to apportion the limits as these have not changed between the two financial years.

If the augmented profits are below the lower limit no apportionment is necessary at all as the SPR has not changed, simply apply the SPR to the whole of the taxable total profits as normal.

Task 5

Frances Ltd makes up accounts to 31 December each year. The following information applies to the year ended 31 December 2014.

	£
Taxable total profits	1,240,000
Dividends plus tax credits (gross dividends)	350,000
Augmented profits	1,590,000

The corporation tax liability for the year is:

£ [   ]

SHORT ACCOUNTING PERIODS

We have seen above how to compute a corporation tax liability for a 12 month accounting period. **If an accounting period is shorter than 12 months the lower and upper limits discussed above are reduced proportionately.**

HOW IT WORKS

For the six months to 31 October 2014 Long Ltd had taxable total profits of £40,000 and no dividends received. Compute the corporation tax payable.

First, work out augmented profits as usual:

	£
Taxable total profits	40,000
Dividends received	0
Augmented profits	40,000

Next compare this with the lower limit applicable in the short accounting period:

Lower limit   £300,000 × 6/12 = £150,000

As augmented profits are below the lower limit the small profits rate of tax applies:

CT liability (FY14) £40,000 × 20% = £ 8,000

Note: All six months fell into FY14, so there was no need to apportion the taxable total profits (and in any case, the taxable total profits were taxed at the small profits rate which has not changed from FY13 to FY14).

If the accounting period is short, and the augmented profits fall between the time-apportioned (the reduced) upper and lower limits, marginal relief will apply. In the marginal relief calculation, the upper limit used is the reduced upper limit.

Task 6

A Ltd had taxable total profits of £200,000 in the nine month accounting period to 31 December 2014. The company received dividends of £45,000 in this period.

(1)   A Ltd's augmented profits for the period ended 31 December 2014 are:

£ [   ]

(2)   The lower limit applicable is:

£ [   ]

and the upper limit applicable is:

£ [   ]

(3)   A Ltd's corporation tax liability for the nine month period to 31 December 2014 is:

£ [   ]

ASSOCIATED COMPANIES

The term ASSOCIATED COMPANY in tax has no connection with financial accounting.

For tax purposes **a company is associated with another company if it either controls the other or if both are under the control of the same person or persons** (individuals, partnerships or companies).

If a company has associated companies, then the above limits need to be 'shared' between all the companies that are associated with each other. This means the upper and lower limits are divided by the number of associated companies + 1 (for the company itself).

Companies that have only been associated for part of an accounting period are deemed to have been associated for the whole period for the purpose of determining these limits.

An associated company is ignored for these purposes if it has not carried on any trade or business at any time in the accounting period (or the part of the period during which it was associated). This means that you should ignore dormant companies. However, you should include non UK companies.

When working out augmented profits any dividends received from associated companies are ignored. You should assume dividends received are not from associated companies unless specifically told otherwise.

HOW IT WORKS

For the year to 31 March 2015, T Ltd, a company with one associated company, has the following results:

	£
Taxable total profits	330,000
Dividend received	45,000

First compute augmented profits

	£
Taxable total profits	330,000
Dividends £45,000 × 100/90	50,000
Augmented profits	380,000

Next compare augmented profits to the lower and upper limits:

Lower limit	£300,000/2	= £150,000
Upper limit	£1,500,000/2	= £750,000

The limits are divided by two as there are two companies that are associated with each other.

As augmented profits are between these limits, marginal relief applies:

	£
FY14	
£330,000 × 21%	69,300
Less small profits marginal relief	
$1/400 \; £(750,000 - 380,000) \times \dfrac{330,000}{380,000}$	(803)
	68,497

As in the case of limits reduced for a short accounting period, the upper limit used in the marginal relief calculation is the reduced upper limit.

Task 7

S Ltd, a company with two associated companies, had taxable total profits of £360,000 in the year to 31 March 2015. Dividends of £22,500 were received in the year.

(1)   S Ltd's augmented profits for the year ended 31 March 2015 are:

£ [   ]

(2)   The lower limit applicable is:

£ [   ]

and the upper limit applicable is:

£ [   ]

(3)   S Ltd's corporation tax liability for the year to 31 March 2015 is:

£ [   ]

COMPANY TAX RETURN FORM

In your assessment you may be asked to complete an extract of the company tax return. A copy of the tax calculation page is available at the end of this chapter.

Generally you will not be expected to complete the whole page, with Tasks either covering boxes 1 – 37 or boxes 38 – 56.

Have a good look at it now to familiarise yourself with the boxes, then you will be able to practise completing this form in the Business Tax Question Bank.

Assessment focus

In the live assessment you will be provided with 'Taxation Data' that can be accessed through pop up windows. The content of these taxation data tables has been reproduced at the front of this Text.

The rates of tax, the upper and lower limits, the standard fraction and the marginal relief formula covered in this chapter are included within 'taxation data 2'. Make sure you familiarise yourself with the content and practise referring to it as you work through this Text.

***For AQ2013** – The information included in this chapter typically will be tested in the following tasks:*

Task 4 – Taxable total profits and corporation tax payable

Task 8 – Tax returns

Performance feedback

The feedback given below relates to students' performance on the AQ2010 version of the assessments. However, the points made by the assessor will be equally as valid for students who will be sitting the assessment under AQ2013.

Task 2.8 (AQ2010)

'Marginal relief has always been an area for confusion for students, so the expectation was that by providing the formula format, student performance in this topic would be much improved. However it should be reported this is not the case.

Other common mistakes are using the net dividends or the gross dividends as the 'N' figure, instead of using taxable total profits. Correctly showing the 'U' figure (upper limit) is also an issue. Too many students divide £1,500,000 by the number of associates, hence failing to add the actual company in.

Adding the marginal relief is a also frequent error.

Inaccurate answers are common such as one student who gave the answer that the upper limit of marginal relief for a six month period and with three associates was £750,000. The corresponding lower limit was also £175,000, apparently.

As this is a key topic, students must ensure that they practice these style questions many times over before attempting the assessment.

Task 2.10 (AQ2010)

The relevant page from the CT600 form for limited companies has been split in two: boxes 1 to 37 are together, and then boxes 38 to 56 are together. Taking the first one of these, in general this return is completed well. Careful reading of the narrative of each box is simply required to ensure that this return is accurately completed.

The completion of the second form fares less well, with students struggling to fully understand what needs to be done. Whilst it is a very short form, it seems that students are simply not practising this return often enough before entering the assessment.

CHAPTER OVERVIEW

- The rate of corporation tax due in a Financial Year depends on the level of a company's augmented profits

- Augmented profits need to be compared with the upper and lower limits to determine the appropriate rate

- Tax may be due at the main rate or the small profits rate. Marginal relief applies when augmented profits are between the upper and lower limits

- Reduce the limits proportionately in short accounting periods

- Divide the limits by the number of associated companies + 1 (for the company itself)

- As corporation tax rates changed between FY13 and FY14 there is a need to split a year straddling 31 March 2014 when calculating the corporation tax liability

Keywords

A **Financial Year** – runs from 1 April to the following 31 March and is identified by the calendar year in which it begins

Augmented profits – are taxable total profits plus the grossed-up amount of dividends received from other (non associated) companies

A **company is associated** – with another company if either controls the other or if both are under the control of the same person or persons (individuals, partnerships or companies)

TEST YOUR LEARNING

Test 1

S Ltd, a company with no associated companies, had taxable total profits of £255,000 for its six month accounting period to 31 March 2015. No dividends were paid or received in the period.

Its corporation tax liability for the period will be:

£ [   ]

Test 2

G Ltd, a company with no associated companies, made up accounts for the nine month period to 31 December 2014. The augmented profits for this period were £55,000, including £5,000 of gross dividends.

The corporation tax liability for the period is:

£ [   ]

Test 3

J Ltd, a company with no associated companies, had taxable total profits of £490,000 in the year ended 31 December 2014. No dividends were received in the year.

The corporation tax liability for the year is:

£ [   ]

Test 4

S Ltd, a company with one associated company, had taxable total profits of £180,000 for the nine month period to 31 March 2015.

Its corporation tax liability for the year will be:

£ [   ]

Test 5

Decide whether the following statement is True or False.

Financial Year 2014 (FY14) begins on 1 April 2014 and ends on 31 March 2015. Tick ONE box

	✓
True	
False	

Page 2

Company tax calculation

Turnover

1	Total turnover from trade or profession	**1** £

Income

3	Trading and professional profits	**3** £
4	Trading losses brought forward claimed against profits	**4** £
5	Net trading and professional profits	*box 3 minus box 4* **5** £
6	Bank, building society or other interest, and profits and gains from non-trading loan relationships	**6** £
11	Income from UK land and buildings	**11** £
14	Annual profits and gains not falling under any other heading	**14** £

Chargeable gains

16	Gross chargeable gains	**16** £
17	Allowable losses including losses brought forward	**17** £
18	Net chargeable gains	*box 16 minus box 17* **18** £
21	**Profits before other deductions and reliefs**	*sum of boxes 5, 6, 11, 14 & 18* **21** £

Deductions and Reliefs

24	Management expenses under S75 ICTA 1988	**24** £
30	Trading losses of this or a later accounting period under S393A ICTA 1988	**30** £
31	Put an 'X' in box 31 if amounts carried back from later accounting periods are included in box 30	**31**
32	Non-trade capital allowances	**32** £
35	Charges paid	**35** £
37	**Taxable total profits**	*box 21 minus boxes 24, 30, 32 and 35* **37** £

Tax calculation

38	Franked investment income	**38** £
39	Number of associated companies in this period or	**39**
40	Associated companies in the first financial year	**40**
41	Associated companies in the second financial year	**41**
42	Put an 'X' in box 42 if the company claims to be charged at the starting rate or the small companies' rate on any part of its profits, or is claiming marginal rate relief	**42**

Enter how much profit has to be charged and at what rate of tax

Financial year *(yyyy)*	Amount of profit	Rate of tax	Tax
43	**44** £	**45**	**46** £ p
53	**54** £	**55**	**56** £ p

63	Corporation tax	*total of boxes 46 and 56* **63** £ p
64	Marginal rate relief	**64** £ p
65	Corporation tax net of marginal rate relief	**65** £ p
66	Underlying rate of corporation tax	**66** • %
67	Profits matched with non-corporate distributions	**67**
68	Tax at non-corporate distributions rate	**68** £ p
69	Tax at underlying rate on remaining profits	**69** £ p
70	**Corporation tax chargeable**	*See note for box 70 in CT600 Guide* **70** £ p

CT600 (Short) (2008) Version 2

chapter 8:
LOSSES

chapter coverage 📖

So far in this Text we have seen how to compute taxable trading profits. Sometimes the result of this computation is a loss rather than a profit. Taxpayers can obtain relief for such a loss, but we will see that the rules for unincorporated businesses are different to those for a company.

In this chapter we start by covering the various methods by which an individual taxpayer may obtain relief for a trading loss, then move on to methods by which a company may obtain relief. We also look at how relief is given for non-trading losses.

The topics we shall cover are:

✍ Trading losses

✍ Unincorporated trade losses

- Relief against income

- Relief against capital gains

✍ Corporation tax losses

- Relief against future trading income

- Relief against total profits

✍ Relieving non-trading losses

✍ Choosing loss relief

TRADING LOSSES

We know the starting point for computing a business' trading results is to take the statement of profit or loss and adjust it for tax purposes. If this adjusted figure is negative then there is a trading loss rather than a taxable profit.

Note that the deduction of capital allowances can actually increase an adjusted loss, or even turn an adjusted profit into a trading loss.

If there is a trading loss, the **taxable trading figure in the relevant tax computation will be NIL**, it is not the negative amount.

- If the trading loss is that of an individual (including partners), the loss will be allocated to a **tax year** using the basis period rules, and the **trading profit for that tax year will be NIL.**

- If the trading loss is incurred by a limited company in an **accounting period,** the **trading profit for that accounting period will be NIL**.

Note: Losses in a partnership are allocated to the partners in the same way as profits. Each partner will then decide on the best method of relief for his share of the loss.

UNINCORPORATED TRADE LOSSES

As we have seen, the trading loss for an unincorporated business is allocated to a tax year in the normal way and the amount taxable in that year is NIL.

HOW IT WORKS

If a trader makes a loss of £5,000 in the year to 31 December 2014, the **2014/15** taxable profits based on that period will be **£nil.**

There will be a trading loss in **2014/15** of £5,000.

The taxpayer has a choice as to how this loss is relieved as follows:

- Carry forward of losses against future trading income
- Losses set against income in the tax year of the loss
- Losses set against income of the previous tax year
- Losses set against capital gains

Relief against income

The taxpayer can choose to relieve the 2014/15 trading loss against income in alternative ways as follows:

(a) **The loss can be carried forward and deducted from taxable trading profits arising from the same trade in future years.** If this option is chosen the loss must be used as quickly as possible. If the following year's taxable trading profits are less than the amount of the loss, then those profits will be reduced to Nil and the balance of the loss will be carried forward to relieve trading profits in future years. The loss can be carried forward indefinitely until it is relieved.

(b) **The loss can be deducted from total income in the tax year of the loss.** You can refer back to the example of an income tax computation in Chapter 1. You will see that total income is the total of a taxpayer's income from all sources. Consequently total income may include rental income, employment income, interest and dividends.

(c) Whether or not option (b) is chosen, **the loss can be deducted from total income in the tax year preceding the tax year of the loss.**

Method (b) and method (c) above are optional reliefs. A taxpayer does not have to deduct a loss under either method if he does not wish to do so. If he does wish to make either of these deductions he would need to make a claim to do so.

If a taxpayer has sufficient loss to deduct under both (b) and (c) he can choose to make one or both of the deductions. **He can also choose the order of the deductions.** However, once a claim is made all of the available loss must be deducted. **Partial claims are not possible.**

Any loss remaining after any claims under (b) and (c) above have been made, is **automatically carried forward** to deduct under (a) against the **first available future trading profits.**

HOW IT WORKS

Ahmed, a sole trader, has the following taxable trading profits/(loss):

	£
Year to 30 September 2013 (and so taxed in 2013/14)	10,000
Year to 30 September 2014 (loss, trading profits = nil in 2014/15)	(49,000)
Year to 30 September 2015 (and so taxed in 2015/16)	20,000

His only other income is rental income of £15,000 a year.

The loss of £49,000 is a loss of **2014/15** and could be deducted from

- **Total income** of £25,000 (trading income of £10,000 + rental income of £15,000) in **2013/14**

- From **total income** (rental income) of £15,000 in **2014/15**

If both of these claims are made, the loss remaining unrelieved of £9,000 is automatically deducted from the **taxable trading profits** of £20,000 arising in **2015/16**.

Claiming to relieve the loss against total income of the current year and the prior year is optional. If he chooses not make a claim to deduct the loss from total income, the loss is carried forward to deduct from taxable trading profits in future years.

The disadvantage of deducting a loss from total income in the year of the loss and/or in the preceding year is that **personal allowances may be wasted**. You will recall that every individual has a personal allowance that he can set against his net income. Income of up to the personal allowance is effectively tax free income so there is no benefit if the net income is reduced to an amount less than the personal allowance.

HOW IT WORKS

Sase has a loss in her period of account ending 31 December 2014 of £13,000. In the year to 31 December 2013 she made a profit of £10,000. Her other income is £9,000 a year and she wishes to claim loss relief for the year of loss and then for the preceding year.

Assuming that the personal allowance was £10,000 in both 2013/14 and 2014/15, Sase's taxable income for each year is calculated in the following way.

The loss-making period ends in 2014/15, so the year of the loss is 2014/15. The trading profit of £10,000 for the year to 31 December 2013 is taxed in 2013/14.

	2013/14	2014/15
	£	£
Trading profits	10,000	NIL
Other income	9,000	9,000
Total income	19,000	9,000
Less loss relief	(4,000)	(9,000)
Net income	15,000	NIL

You can see that in 2014/15, Sase's personal allowance will be wasted. If Sase claims loss relief in this year there is nothing she can do about this waste of relief. Alternatively, Sase could make the 2013/14 claim and not the 2014/15 claim. This would leave net income of £6,000 in 2013/14 to set the personal allowance against, with the remainder of the personal allowance in 2013/14 wasted. The total income in 2014/15 would be covered by the personal allowance that year.

Task 1

In 2014/15 Niahla makes a loss of £30,000. Her total income in 2014/15 is £21,000, and her personal allowance for that year is £10,000. She has no other source of income for any other year. If she obtains loss relief as soon as possible, the loss carried forward for future relief is:

£ [   ]

Relief against capital gains

Where relief is claimed against total income of a given year (in the income tax computation), the taxpayer may include a **further claim to set the loss against chargeable gains for the year** less any allowable capital losses for the year or for previous years. This amount of net gains is computed ignoring the annual exempt amount. We will see what is meant by this in Chapter 12, when we look at chargeable gains.

The trading loss is first set against total income of the year of the claim, and only any excess loss is set against capital gains. The taxpayer cannot specify the amount to set against, so the annual exempt amount may be wasted. An example is included here for completeness. We will study chargeable gains later in this Text and it is suggested that you revisit this example at that point.

HOW IT WORKS

Guy has the following results for 2014/15

	2014/15 £
Trading loss	27,000
Total income	19,500
Capital gains less current year capital losses	14,000
Annual exempt amount	11,000

The loss would be relieved against income and gains as follows:

Income tax computation 2014/15	£
Total income	19,500
Less current year loss relief	(19,500)
Net income	0
Personal allowance (wasted)	

Capital gains tax computation 2014/15	£
Current year gains less current year losses	14,000
Less relief for trading loss	(7,500)
Chargeable gain	6,500
Annual exempt amount (partly wasted)	(6,500)
Taxable gain	0

CORPORATION TAX LOSSES

As we mentioned above if the trading loss is incurred by a limited company in an **accounting period,** the trading profit for that accounting period will be NIL.

You need to be aware of the following three methods by which a company may obtain relief for its trading losses:

(a) Carry forward against future trading profits
(b) Set-off against current profits
(c) Carry back against earlier profits

You will also need to be aware of the impact losses can have on qualifying charitable donations. This is included within examples and tasks below.

We will look at each of the three methods of obtaining loss relief:

Relief against future trading income

A company can claim to set a trading loss against profits from the same trade in future accounting periods. Relief is given against the first available trading profits from the same trade. This relief is called CARRY FORWARD LOSS RELIEF.

HOW IT WORKS

P Ltd has the following results for the three years to 31 March 2015:

	Year ended 31 March		
	2013 £	2014 £	2015 £
Trading profit/(loss)	(8,000)	3,000	6,000
Bank interest	0	4,000	2,000

Carry forward loss relief would be relieved as follows:

	Year ended 31 March		
	2013 £	2014 £	2015 £
Trading profit	NIL	3,000	6,000
Less carry forward loss relief	–	(3,000) (i)	(5,000) (ii)
Bank interest	–	4,000	2,000
Taxable total profits	NIL	4,000	3,000

Note that the carried forward loss is set against the trading profits only in future years. It cannot be set against other income such as the bank interest.

Task 2

On 1 April 2014 M Ltd had the following amount brought forward:

Trading losses   £50,000

M Ltd's results for the year to 31 March 2015 were:

	£
Trading profits	40,000
Property income	25,000
Chargeable gain	2,000

(1)   The taxable total profits for the year to 31 March 2015 are:

£ [   ]

(2)   What amount, if any, of the trading losses remain to be carried forward at 1 April 2015?

£ [   ]

Relief against total profits

A company may claim to offset a trading loss incurred in an accounting period against total profits (before deducting qualifying charitable donations) of the same accounting period. This relief is called CURRENT PERIOD LOSS RELIEF. Any qualifying charitable donations that become unrelieved, as a result of a current period claim, are lost. **A trading loss that cannot be fully relieved against profits of the same accounting period may then be carried back and relieved against total profits of the twelve months immediately preceding the loss making period.** This relief is called CARRY BACK LOSS RELIEF.

In contrast to the rules for individuals, current period relief must be used in the loss making period **before** carry back loss relief.

Where the loss is being carried back it is set against profits before the deduction of qualifying charitable donations. Any qualifying charitable donations that become unrelieved, as a result of a carry back claim, are lost.

Claims for current period or carry back loss relief cannot specify how much of the loss is to apply and, once made, **must relieve profits to the maximum possible extent.**

Any loss remaining unrelieved after current period and carry back loss relief claims **must be carried forward and set against future profits of the same trade** under carry forward loss relief.

HOW IT WORKS

Patagonia Ltd started trading on 1 August 2012 and has the following results for the first two accounting periods to 31 July 2014:

	Year ended 31 July	
	2013	2014
	£	£
Trading profit (loss)	45,000	(50,000)
Building society interest	400	5,300
Qualifying charitable donations	500	500

Current period and carry back loss relief would be relieved as follows:

	Year ended 31 July	
	2013	2014
	£	£
Trading profit	45,000	NIL
Interest	400	5,300
Total profits	45,400	5,300
Less current period loss relief	–	(5,300)
	45,400	0
Less carry back loss relief	(44,700)	–
Less qualifying charitable donation	(500)	–
Taxable total profits	200	0
Unrelieved qualifying charitable donations	–	500

Task 3

JB Ltd had the following results in the three accounting periods to 31 March 2016:

	Year ended 31 March 2014 £	Year ended 31 March 2015 £	Year ended 31 March 2016 £
Trading profits/(loss)	70,000	(160,000)	60,000
Property income	10,000	10,000	10,000
Qualifying charitable donation	(10,000)	(30,000)	(15,000)

(1) Using the proforma layout provided, show how the trading loss of £160,000 incurred in the year to 31 March 2015 may be relieved. Input 0 if your answer is zero.

	Year ended 31 March 2014 £	Year ended 31 March 2015 £	Year ended 31 March 2016 £
Trading profits			
Less c/fwd loss relief			
Property income			
Total profits			
Less CY and C/B loss relief			
Less qualifying charitable donation			
Taxable total profits			

(2) Complete the following table showing the amount of unrelieved qualifying charitable donation.

	Year ended 31 March 2014 £	Year ended 31 March 2015 £	Year ended 31 March 2016 £
Unrelieved qualifying charitable donation			

(3) The trading loss to carry forward is:

£ [   ]

The carry back loss relief is strictly a 12 month carry back. Therefore if the accounting period before the one of the loss is less than 12 months long, the loss can be carried back to the period before the short period. However, the profits available for relief in that period must be apportioned (on a time basis) to ensure that only 12 months of profits in total have had losses relieved against them.

RELIEVING NON-TRADING LOSSES

Capital losses

We will look at how to calculate capital gains and losses for both individuals and companies in Chapter 12.

The rules for relieving CAPITAL LOSSES are much more restrictive, than those for trading losses.

Capital losses for both individuals and companies can only be **set against current year capital gains,** and any **remaining losses are carried forward and set against future gains.** Capital losses can only be set against gains, never against income, and they cannot be carried back.

We will see in Chapter 12 that individuals pay CAPITAL GAINS TAX on their gains, and we will look at how to deal with capital losses in the capital gains tax computation.

Companies however, pay CORPORATION TAX on any chargeable gains, as they are included in the computation of taxable total profits.

The following Task includes an example of the use of capital losses for a company.

Task 4

Y Ltd had the following results for the three years to 31 October 2014:

	Year ended 31 October		
	2012	*2013*	*2014*
	£	*£*	*£*
Trading profits/(loss)	50,000	40,000	(90,000)
Bank interest	10,000	5,000	5,000
Chargeable gain/(allowable loss)	(7,000)	–	12,000

Using the proforma layout provided, calculate taxable total profits for each year assuming the company makes claims for loss relief as early as possible. Input 0 if your answer is zero.

	Year ended 31 October		
	2012 £	2013 £	2014 £
Trading profits			
Bank interest			
Chargeable gain			
Total profits			
Less current period loss relief			
Less carry back loss relief			
Taxable total profits			

The trading loss to carry forward is:

£

CHOOSING LOSS RELIEF

Individuals

As we have seen above, several alternative loss reliefs may be available for an individual, including

- Carry forward of losses
- Losses set against income in the tax year of the loss
- Losses set against income of the previous tax year
- Losses set against capital gains

In making a choice consider:

(a) **The rate at which relief will be obtained**.

We saw in Chapter one that individuals can pay income tax at the starting rate, the basic rate, the higher rate and the additional rate.

The most beneficial method is to try and offset losses against any income being taxed at the highest rate.

(b) **How quickly relief will be obtained**. It is quicker, and therefore could be more beneficial, to obtain loss relief against income of the previous year and current year rather than wait to carry forward loss relief.

(c) **The extent to which personal allowances and the annual exempt amount might be lost**.

Companies

We have also seen that there are several alternative loss reliefs available for a company, including

- Carry forward of losses
- Losses set against current profits
- Losses set against profits from earlier years

In making a choice consider:

(a) **The rate at which relief will be obtained**:

(i) 21% at the main rate
(ii) 20% at the small profits rate

(b) **How quickly relief will be obtained**: loss relief against total profits is quicker than carry forward loss relief.

(c) **The extent to which relief for qualifying charitable donations might be lost**.

Assessment focus

None of the information in this chapter is included within the 'Taxation Data' available in the live assessment.

The information included in this chapter typically will be tested in the following task:

Task 6 – Losses for sole traders, partnerships and limited companies

Performance feedback

The feedback given below relates to students' performance on the AQ2010 version of the assessments. However, the points made by the assessor will be equally as valid for students sitting the assessment under AQ2013.

Task 1.4 (AQ2010)

The questions can be either written, or computational. This task is the worst answered in Section 1 with only 35% of students achieving 'Met' standard.

It may be assumed that the computational style of question would be better handled than the written style. However, this is simply not the case. **Students will always be instructed on how to offset any loss so they will not need to apply tax planning aspects in any computational questions,** *but following these instructions seems to be an issue. For example, too many students are carrying forward all losses before carrying back, despite the instruction to claim loss relief as early as possible.*

CHAPTER OVERVIEW

- For an individual a trading loss can be

  (a) carried forward to be deducted from the first available profits of the same trade

  (b) deducted from total income in the tax year of the loss and/or in the preceding tax year

  (c) deducted from net gains in the year of the claim

- For a company a trading loss can be

  (a) carried forward and set against future trading profits of the same trade

  (b) deducted from total profits in the accounting period of the loss

  (c) deducted from total profits in the 12 months preceding the period of the loss

- Current period and carry back relief for a company is given against total profits before deducting qualifying charitable donations

- An individual can choose the order in which to claim for current year loss relief and prior year loss relief

- For a company, a claim for current period loss relief must be made before a loss is carried back

- Capital losses can be set against current period gains or carried forward to gains in the future

- When selecting a loss relief, consider the rate at which relief is obtained and the timing of the relief

Keywords

Trading losses – is when the accounting profit is adjusted for tax purposes, and this adjusted figure is negative

Carry forward loss relief – allows both an individual and a company to set a trading loss against the first available profits from the same trade in the future

Current year loss relief – allows a company to set a trading loss against total profits before deducting qualifying charitable donations in the loss making accounting period, and an individual to set a trading loss against total income in the tax year of the loss

Carry back loss relief – allows a company to set a trading loss against total profits (before deducting qualifying charitable donations) in the 12 months preceding the period of the loss, and an individual to set a trading loss against total income in the tax year prior to the tax year of the loss

TEST YOUR LEARNING

Test 1

Harold (a sole trader) who has been in business for many years, makes a trading loss of £20,000 in the year ended 31 January 2015.

In which year(s) may the loss be relieved against total income, assuming relief is claimed as soon as possible? Tick ONE box

	✓
2014/15 only	
2015/16 and/or 2014/15	
2013/14 only	
2014/15 and/or 2013/14	

Test 2

Identify whether the following statement is true of false.

For an individual trading losses can only be carried forward for deduction in the six succeeding tax years.

	✓
True	
False	

Test 3

Where trade losses are carried forward by an individual, against what sort of income may they be relieved? Tick ONE box

	✓
Against non-savings income	
Against total income	
Against trading income arising in the same trade	
Against trading income arising in all trades carried on by the taxpayer	

BPP
LEARNING MEDIA

Test 4

Mallory (a sole trader), who has traded for many years, has the following recent tax adjusted results:

Year ended 30 April 2013	Profit	£10,000
Year ended 30 April 2014	Loss	£(40,000)
Year ended 30 April 2015	Profit	£25,000

Mallory has other income of £9,000 each year. **Explain how the loss in the year to 30 April 2014 can be relieved.**

Test 5

(1)   CR Ltd has the following results for the two years to 31 October 2014:

	Year ended 31 October	
	2013	2014
	£	£
Trading profit (loss)	170,000	(320,000)
Interest	5,000	60,000
Chargeable gain (loss)	(20,000)	12,000
Qualifying charitable donation	5,000	5,000

Calculate the amount of trading loss remaining to be carried forward at 1 November 2014 assuming that all possible loss relief claims against total profits are made?

£	

(2)   **Calculate the amount of capital loss remaining to be carried forward at 1 November 2014?**

£	

Test 6

JB Ltd had the following results in the three accounting periods to 30 September 2014:

	Year ended 31 March 2013 £	Six months to 30 September 2013 £	Year ended 30 September 2014 £
Trading profit/(loss)	4,000	6,000	(10,000)
Qualifying charitable donation	1,000	3,000	1,500

Identify the amount, if any, of the trading loss incurred in the year ended 30 September 2014 that may be relieved against total profits in the year ended 31 March 2013. Tick ONE box

	✓
£Nil	
£2,000	
£4,000	
£3,000	

chapter 9:
NATIONAL INSURANCE

— chapter coverage 📖 —

In previous chapters we have covered income tax for the self employed, and corporation tax for companies.

In this chapter we see that the self employed must also pay two types of National Insurance contribution (NIC). We see how to calculate these contributions.

The topic that we shall cover is:

✍ NICs payable by the self employed

INTRODUCTION

Paying National Insurance contributions (NICs) builds up an individual's entitlement to certain state benefits, such as pensions.

In the Business Tax assessment, you will only need to be aware of the NICs payable by the self employed.

NICS PAYABLE BY THE SELF EMPLOYED

The self employed (ie sole traders and partners) must pay two types of NIC:

(a) CLASS 2 CONTRIBUTIONS
(b) CLASS 4 CONTRIBUTIONS

Class 2 contributions are payable at a flat rate of £2.75 a week. It is possible to be excepted from Class 2 contributions if annual **accounting** profits (rather than taxable profits) are less than £5,885.

An individual who starts to trade must notify HMRC that he is liable to Class 2 contributions. There is a penalty for failure to notify by 31 January following the end of the tax year in which trade started.

Class 4 contributions are based on the level of the individual's trading profits. Main rate contributions are calculated by applying a fixed percentage of 9% (for 2014/15) to the individual's profits between the annual lower profits limit (LPL) of £7,956 (for 2014/15) and the annual upper profits limit (UPL) of £41,865 (for 2014/15).

Additional rate contributions are 2% (for 2014/15) on profits above the annual upper profits limit.

HOW IT WORKS

If Jon had taxable trading profits of £46,000 for 2014/15 his Class 4 liability would be calculated in the following way:

	£
Annual upper profits limit	41,865
Less annual lower profits limit	(7,956)
	33,909

		£
Class 4 NICs =	9% × £33,909	3,051.81
	2% × (46,000 – 41,865)	82.70
Total		3,134.51

In addition Jon would pay Class 2 contributions of (52 × £2.75) = £143.00.

Task 1

Lawrence, who is a sole trader, had taxable profits of £25,000 for 2014/15. The NICs he must pay are:

(Show your answers in pounds and pence).

Class 2

£ [   ] . [   ]

Class 4

£ [   ] . [   ]

Task 2

Amelia had taxable partnership profits of £60,000 for 2014/15.

The NICs she must pay are:

(Show your answers in pounds and pence).

Class 2

£ [   ] . [   ]

Class 4

£ [   ] . [   ]

Assessment focus

In the live assessment you will be provided with 'Taxation Data' that can be accessed through pop up windows. The content of these taxation data tables has been reproduced at the front of this Text.

The rates and limits for Class 2 and Class 4 NICs covered in this chapter are included within 'taxation data 1'. Make sure you familiarise yourself with the content and practise referring to it as you work through this Text.

The information included in this chapter typically will be tested in the following task:

Task 5 – National insurance contributions

Performance feedback

The feedback given below relates to students' performance on the AQ2010 version of the assessments. However, the points made by the assessor will be equally as valid for students who will be sitting the assessment under AQ2013.

Task 2.6 (AQ2010)

National insurance contributions for Class 2 and 4 is the sole topic for this task. Although the third best answered task in Section 2, it is quite amazing how many students fail to gain full marks. As all the rates are in the tax tables, it is quite puzzling how some answers are arrived at.

The vast majority of questions are computational, but the sample assessment for FA11 demonstrates how written questions could look.

Students appear to be losing marks through sheer carelessness, possibly due to their belief that this is an easy topic. Given that 6% of students gained virtually no marks for this task at all, this belief is misplaced.

CHAPTER OVERVIEW

- Self employed traders pay

  (a) Class 2 contributions at a flat rate per week of £2.75 (in 2014/15), and
  (b) Class 4 contributions based on the level of their profits

- Main rate Class 4 NICs are 9% of profits between the UPL and LPL

- Additional Class 4 NICs are 2% of profits above the UPL

Keywords

Class 2 contributions – are flat rate contributions payable by the self employed

Class 4 contributions – are profit related contributions payable by the self employed

TEST YOUR LEARNING

Compute the following total sole traders' liabilities to NICs for 2014/15.

Test 1

Acker

Taxable trading profits and accounting profits   £5,050

£		.	

Test 2

Bailey

Taxable trading profits   £50,000

£		.	

Test 3

Cartwright

Taxable trading profits   £10,850

£		.	

chapter 10:
SELF ASSESSMENT FOR INDIVIDUALS

chapter coverage 📖

In this chapter we look at when tax returns must be filed, for how long records must be kept and the penalties chargeable for failure to comply with the requirements.

We then look at the due dates for payment of income tax and the consequences of late payment.

Finally, we complete the chapter considering the powers of HMRC to enquire into a return.

The topics covered are:

- Tax returns and keeping records
- Penalties
- Payment of tax, interest and penalties for late payment
- Compliance checks and enquiries

TAX RETURNS AND KEEPING RECORDS

An individual's tax return comprises a Tax Form, together with supplementary pages for particular sources of income and capital gains. **We will look at self assessment of income tax in this Chapter**. The self assessment of capital gains is very similar but we will consider it in detail later in Chapter 12 of this Text.

Notice of chargeability

Individuals who are chargeable to tax for any tax year and who have not received a notice to file a return are, in general, required to **give notice of chargeability within six months from the end of the tax year**, ie by 5 October 2015 for 2014/15.

Filing tax returns

The FILING DUE DATE is:

- For paper returns – **31 October following the end of the tax year** that the return covers, eg for 2014/15 by 31 October 2015.

- For returns filed online – **31 January following the end of the tax year** that the return covers, eg for 2014/15 by 31 January 2016.

Where a notice to make a return is issued after 31 July following the tax year a period of three months is allowed for the filing of a paper return.

Where a notice to make a return is issued after 31 October following the tax year a period of three months is allowed for the online filing of that return.

An individual may ask HMRC to make the tax computation if a paper return is filed. Where an online return is filed, the tax computation is made automatically.

HOW IT WORKS

Advise the following clients of the latest filing date for their personal tax return for 2014/15 if notice to file the return is received on the following dates and the return is:

(a)   Paper
(b)   Online

Notice to file tax return issued by HMRC:

Norma	on 6 April 2015
Melanie	on 10 August 2015
Olga	on 12 December 2015

The latest filing dates are:

	Paper	**Online**
Norma	31 October 2015	31 January 2016
Melanie	9 November 2015	31 January 2016
Olga	11 March 2016	11 March 2016

Task 1

HMRC issued a notice to file a tax return for 2014/15 to Myer on 3 November 2015. She filed this return online on 31 March 2016. State the date by which the return should have been filed:

Keeping of records

Taxpayers must keep and retain all records required to enable them to make and deliver a correct tax return.

In general, records must be retained by tax payers until the later of:

(a)   **One year after the 31 January following the tax year** concerned

(b)   **Five years after 31 January following the tax year** concerned if the taxpayer is in **business or has property business income**

PENALTIES

Penalties for errors in the return

A penalty may be imposed where a taxpayer makes an inaccurate return if he has:

(a) **Been careless** because he has not taken reasonable care in making the return or discovers the error later but does not take reasonable steps to inform HMRC

(b) **Made a deliberate error** but does not make arrangements to conceal it

(c) **Made a deliberate error and has attempted to conceal it**, eg by submitting false evidence in support of an inaccurate figure

An error which is made where the taxpayer has taken reasonable care in making the return and which he does not discover later, does not result in a penalty.

In order for a penalty to be charged, the inaccurate return must result in:

(a) An understatement of the taxpayer's tax liability
(b) A false or increased loss for the taxpayer
(c) A false or increased repayment of tax to the taxpayer

If a return contains more than one error, a penalty can be charged for each error. The rules also extend to errors in claims for allowances and reliefs and in accounts submitted in relation to tax liability.

The amount of the penalty for error is based on the Potential Lost Revenue (PLR) to HMRC as a result of the error. For example, if there is an understatement of tax, this understatement will be the PLR.

The maximum amount of the penalty for error depends on the type of error.

Type of error	Maximum penalty payable
Mistake	No penalty
Careless	30% of PLR
Deliberate but not concealed	70% of PLR
Deliberate and concealed	100% of PLR

A penalty for error may be reduced if the taxpayer tells HMRC about the error – this is called a disclosure. The reduction depends on the circumstances of the disclosure and the help that the taxpayer gives to HMRC in relation to the disclosure.

An unprompted disclosure is one made at a time when the taxpayer has no reason to believe HMRC has discovered, or is about to discover, the error. Otherwise, the disclosure will be a **prompted disclosure**. The minimum penalties that can be imposed are as follows.

Type of error	'Unprompted'	'Prompted'
Careless	0% of PLR	15% of PLR
Deliberate but not concealed	20% of PLR	35% of PLR
Deliberate and concealed	30% of PLR	50% of PLR

You will see that an unprompted disclosure where a careless mistake has been made can reduce a penalty for error to nil and all penalties can be reduced by half if the taxpayer makes a prompted disclosure.

A penalty for a careless error may be suspended by HMRC to allow the taxpayer to take action to ensure that the error does not occur again (eg where the error has arisen from failure to keep proper records).

HMRC will impose conditions which the taxpayer has to satisfy, eg establishing proper recordkeeping systems.

The penalty will be cancelled if the conditions imposed by HMRC are complied with by the taxpayer within a period of up to two years.

A taxpayer can appeal against:

(a) The penalty being charged
(b) The amount of the penalty
(c) A decision by HMRC not to suspend a penalty
(d) The conditions set by HMRC in relation to the suspension of a penalty

Task 2

Kelly deliberately omitted an invoice from her trading income in her 2014/15 tax return, but did not destroy the evidence. She later disclosed this error, before she had reason to believe HMRC might investigate the matter.

Complete the following sentence:

Kelly's penalty can be reduced from ☐ % of the potential lost revenue (for a deliberate, but not concealed error) to ☐ %, with the unprompted disclosure of her error.

Penalties for late notification

A penalty can be charged for failure to notify chargeability to income tax and/or capital gains tax. Penalties are behaviour related, increasing for more serious failures, and are again based on 'potential lost revenue'. This time the PLR is the income tax or capital gains tax which is unpaid on 31 January following the tax year.

The minimum and maximum penalties as percentages of PLR are as follows:

Behaviour	Maximum penalty	Minimum penalty with unprompted disclosure		Minimum penalty with prompted disclosure	
Deliberate and concealed	100%	30%		50%	
Deliberate but not concealed	70%	20%		35%	
		≥ 12m	<12m	≥12m	<12m
Careless	30%	10%	0%	20%	10%

There is no zero penalty for reasonable care (as there is for penalties for errors on returns – see above), although the penalty may be reduced to 0% if the failure is rectified within 12 months through unprompted disclosure. The penalties may also be reduced at HMRC's discretion in 'special circumstances'. Inability to pay the penalty is not a 'special circumstance'.

The same penalties apply for failure to notify HMRC of a new taxable activity.

Where the taxpayer's failure is not 'deliberate', there is no penalty if he can show he has a 'reasonable excuse'. Reasonable excuse does not include having insufficient money to pay the penalty. Taxpayers can appeal against penalty decisions.

Penalties for late filing

The penalties for filing a late tax return are:

(a) **Immediate £100 penalty** (even if no tax is owing).

(b) **A daily penalty of £10 may be levied** if the return is more than 3 months late (up to maximum 90 days).

(c) **5% of the tax due** if the return is more than 6 months but less than 12 months late.

(d) If the return is more than 12 months late the penalty is

- **100% of the tax due** where withholding of information is **deliberate and concealed**.

- **70% of the tax due** where withholding of information is **deliberate but not concealed**.

- **5% of the tax due** in other cases (eg **careless**).

These tax based penalties (c and d above) are all subject to a minimum of £300.

Penalties for failure to keep records

The maximum penalty for each failure to keep and retain records is **£3,000** per tax year.

PAYMENT OF TAX, INTEREST AND PENALTIES FOR LATE PAYMENT

Payments of tax

A taxpayer must usually make **three payments of income tax and Class 4 NICs:**

Date	Payment
31 January in the tax year	First payment on account
31 July after the tax year	Second payment on account
31 January after the tax year	Final payment to settle any remaining liability

Each PAYMENT ON ACCOUNT is equal to 50% of the income tax payable (after the deduction of PAYE and tax suffered at source) plus Class 4 NICs for the previous year.

Class 2 NICs can be collected monthly or twice yearly by direct debit, or paid twice yearly in response to requests issued by HMRC. Monthly direct debits are collected four months in arrears, so payments for 2014/15 would start in August 2014. Half yearly payments are due by 31 January during the tax year and 31 July after the end of the tax year. So for 2014/15, the first six months worth of Class 2 NICs would be paid by 31 January 2015 and the second six months worth by 31 July 2015. Payment by direct debit, as opposed to in response to a request from HMRC, would therefore ensure these deadlines are met.

Capital gains tax must all be paid on 31 January following the tax year. There are no payments on account of capital gains tax. We will see this in more detail in Chapter 12 of this Text.

HOW IT WORKS

Jeremy's income tax payable and Class 4 NICs for 2014/15 totalled £12,000.

Each payment on account for 2015/16 is £12,000/2 = £6,000.

Task 3

Karen's income tax payable and Class 4 NICs for 2014/15 totalled £14,000. She estimates that her income tax payable and Class 4 NICs for 2015/16 will be £16,000.

Complete the following:

Each payment on account for 2015/16 will be

They will be due on

and

Payments on account are not required if the income tax payable for the previous year is less than £1,000, or if more than 80% of the previous year's liability was paid by tax deducted at source.

Payments on account are normally fixed by reference to the previous year's income tax payable but if a taxpayer expects his tax payable to be lower than this he may claim to reduce his payments on account to:

(a)   A stated amount
(b)   Nil

If the taxpayer's eventual tax payable is higher than he estimated (after making such a claim) he will have reduced the payments on account too far. Although the payments on account will not be adjusted, the taxpayer will suffer an interest charge on late payment.

The balance of any income tax is normally payable on or before the 31 January following the tax year.

HOW IT WORKS

Jameel made payments on account for 2014/15 of £7,500 each on 31 January 2015 and 31 July 2015, based on his 2013/14 tax payable. He later calculates his total income tax payable for 2014/15 at £20,000.

The final payment for 2014/15 is £20,000 – £7,500 – £7,500 = £5,000.

In one case the due date for the final payment is later than 31 January following the end of the tax year. If a taxpayer has notified chargeability by 5 October but

the notice to file a tax return is not issued before 31 October, then the due date for the final payment is three months after the issue of the notice.

Penalties for late payment of tax

Penalties for late payment of tax will be imposed in respect of balancing payments of income tax.

A penalty is chargeable where tax is paid after the penalty date. **The penalty date is 30 days after the due date for tax.** Therefore no penalty arises if the tax is paid within 30 days of the due date.

Date of payment	Penalty
Not more than 5 months after the penalty date:	5% of unpaid tax
More than 5 months but not more than 11 months after the penalty date:	10% of unpaid tax
More than 11 months after the penalty date:	15% of unpaid tax

Penalties for late payment of tax **apply to balancing payments** of income tax. They **do not apply to late payments on account**.

Interest

INTEREST is chargeable on **late payment of both payments on account and balancing payments**. In both cases interest runs from the **due date until the day before the actual date of payment.**

If a taxpayer claims to reduce his payments on account and there is still a final payment to be made, interest is normally charged on the payments on account as if each of those payments had been the lower of:

(a) The reduced amount, plus 50% of the final income tax payable

(b) The amount which would have been payable had no claim for reduction been made

HOW IT WORKS

Harry made two payments on account of £2,500 each for 2014/15. The payments were made on 31 January 2015 and 31 July 2015. Harry had claimed to reduce these payments from the £4,000 that would have been due had they been based on his previous year's income tax payable.

Harry's 2014/15 tax return showed that his income tax payable for 2014/15 (before deducting payments on account) was £10,000. Harry paid the balance of income tax due of £5,000 on 30 September 2016.

Harry will be charged interest as follows:

The payments on account should have been £4,000 each. Interest will therefore be charged on the £1,500 not paid on 31 January 2015, from that date until the day before payment (29 September 2016). Similarly, interest will run on the other £1,500 that should have been paid on 31 July 2015 until the day before payment 29 September 2016.

The final balancing payment should have been £2,000 (£10,000 – £8,000). Interest will run on £2,000 from the due date of 31 January 2016 until the day before payment 29 September 2016.

Note. There would also be a late payment penalty of 10% due on the actual balancing payment of £5,000 (more than 6 months late).

Repayment of tax and repayment interest

Tax is repaid when claimed unless a greater payment of tax is due in the following 30 days, in which case it is set-off against that payment.

REPAYMENT INTEREST is paid on overpayments of:

(a) Payments on account
(b) Final payments of income tax
(c) Penalties

Repayment interest runs from the **later of the date of overpayment or the date the tax was due until the day before the tax is repaid.** Tax deducted at source is treated as if it had been paid on the 31 January following the end of the tax year.

COMPLIANCE CHECKS AND ENQUIRIES

HMRC has the power to conduct a COMPLIANCE CHECK into an individual's tax return.

Some returns are selected for a compliance check at random, others for a particular reason, for example, if HMRC believes that there has been an underpayment of tax due to the taxpayer's failure to comply with tax legislation.

There are two different types of compliance check:

■ Pre-return checks, which are conducted using its information powers

- Enquiries into returns, claims or elections which have already been submitted

Examples of when a pre-return check may be carried out in practice include:

- To assist with clearances or ruling requests

- Where a previous check has identified poor record-keeping

- To check that computer systems will produce the information needed to support a return

- To find out about planning or avoidance schemes

- Where fraud is suspected

Notice must be given by HMRC of the intention to conduct an enquiry by:

- The first anniversary of the actual filing date

- If the return is filed after the due filing date, the quarter day following the first anniversary of the actual filing date. The quarter days are 31 January, 30 April, 31 July and 31 October

HMRC has only one opportunity to open a formal enquiry and a tax return cannot be subject to a formal enquiry more than once.

In the course of the enquiries the taxpayer may be required to produce documents, accounts or other information. The taxpayer can appeal to the Tax tribunal against this.

HMRC must issue a closure notice when the enquiries are complete, state the conclusions and amend the self-assessment accordingly. If the taxpayer is not satisfied with the amendment he may, within 30 days, appeal to the Tax Tribunal.

Assessment focus

None of the information in this chapter is included within the 'Taxation Data' which you will be provided with in the live assessment.

The information included in this chapter typically will be tested in the following task:

Task 7 – Payments on account and penalties.

Performance feedback

The feedback given below relates to students' performance on the AQ2010 version of the assessments. However, the points made by the assessor will be equally as valid for students sitting the assessment under AQ2013.

Task 2.7 (AQ2010)

There are two main topics assessable within this task - self assessment, including payments on account and balancing payments; and capital gains tax payable for individuals.

These appear to be quite straightforward areas of the standards, but only 50% of students achieved competence. It is the self-assessment amounts of tax payable that cause the most issues.

Task 2.9 (AQ2010)

It may be no surprise that this task is the second most poorly performed one in Section 2. Penalties and interest for both individuals and companies is assessable, mainly covering errors and late payment of tax. This is not the exhaustive list, but these areas would be expected in some detail in every question.

CHAPTER OVERVIEW

- A tax return must be filed by 31 January following a tax year provided it is filed online. Paper returns must be filed by 31 October following the tax year

- Taxpayers must keep records until the later of:
  - (a) One year after the 31 January following the tax year
  - (b) Five years after the 31 January following the tax year if in business or with property income

- A penalty may be imposed if the taxpayer makes an error in his tax return based on the Potential Lost Revenue as a result of the error

- A penalty may be imposed if the taxpayer does not notify HMRC of his liability to pay income tax or capital gains tax. The penalty is based on Potential Lost Revenue.

- A fixed penalty of £100 applies if a return is filed late; followed by a potential daily penalty of £10 if the return is filed between three and six months late

- A tax-geared penalty will also apply if a return is filed more than six months late, with a further penalty if this is over twelve months late

- Payments on account of income tax are required on 31 January in the tax year and on 31 July following the tax year

- Balancing payments of income tax are due on 31 January following the tax year

- Late payment penalties apply to balancing payments of income tax. They do not apply to late payments on account

- Interest is chargeable on late payment of both payments on account and balancing payments

- HMRC can enquire into a return, usually within one year of receipt of the return

Keywords

Filing due date – the date by which a return must be filed

Payment on account – an amount paid on account of income tax and Class 4 NIC

Interest – charged on late payments on account and on late balancing payments

Repayment interest – payable by HMRC on overpaid payments on account, balancing payments and penalties

TEST YOUR LEARNING

Test 1

The due filing date for an income tax return for 2014/15 assuming the taxpayer will submit the return online is (insert date as XX/XX/XX):

[   ]

Test 2

Select the correct answers from the pick lists provided

The 2014/15 payments on account will be calculated as

[   ]

of the income tax payable and Class 4 NICs for

[   ]

and will be due on

[   ]

and

[   ]

Pick list 1	Pick list 2	Pick list 3	Pick list 4
50%	2014/15	1 January 2016	31 July 2015
25%	2013/14	1 January 2015	31 December 2015
100%	2015/16	31 January 2015	31 January 2016

Test 3

A notice requiring a tax return for 2014/15 is issued in April 2015 and the return is filed online in May 2016. All income tax was paid in May 2016. No payments on account were due.

Explain what charges will be made on the taxpayer.

Test 4

Susie filed her 2014/15 tax return online on 28 January 2016.

By what date must HMRC give notice that they are going to enquire into the return? Tick ONE box

	✓
31 January 2017	
31 March 2017	
6 April 2017	
28 January 2017	

Test 5

Jamie paid income tax of £12,000 for 2013/14. In 2014/15, his tax payable was £16,000.

Jamie's 2014/15 payments on account will each be

and will be due on (insert date as XX/XX/XX)

and

Jamie's balancing payment will be

and will be due on (insert date as XX/XX/XX)

Test 6

Tim should have made two payments on account of his 2014/15 income tax payable of £5,000 each. He actually made both of these payments on 31 August 2015.

State the amount of any penalties for late payment.

£	

Test 7

(1) **By what date must a taxpayer generally submit a tax return for 2014/15 if it is filed as a paper return?**

	✓
30 September 2015	
31 October 2015	
31 December 2015	
31 January 2016	

(2) **On which dates are payment on accounts due for 2014/15?**

	✓
31 January 2016 and 31 July 2016	
31 January 2015 and 31 July 2015	
31 October 2015 and 31 January 2016	
31 July 2015 and 31 January 2016	

Test 8

Lola accidentally fails to include an invoice of £17,000 on her 2014/15 tax return. She pays basic rate tax at 20%, and has not yet disclosed this error.

Identify the maximum penalty that could be imposed on her. Tick ONE box

	✓
£5,100	
£3,400	
£1,020	
£2,380	

chapter 11:
SELF ASSESSMENT FOR COMPANIES

chapter coverage 📖

In this chapter we look at when corporation tax returns must be filed, for how long records must be kept and the penalties chargeable for failure to comply with the requirements.

We then look at the due dates for payment of corporation tax and the consequences of late payment.

The topics that we shall cover are:

✍ Notification of chargeability

✍ Company tax returns and keeping records

✍ Payment of tax and interest

NOTIFICATION OF CHARGEABILITY

A company must notify HMRC when it first comes within the scope of corporation tax. This will usually be when it starts trading. There is a list of information that needs to be included in the notice, which must be given in writing. **The notice must be made within three months**.

A company which is chargeable to tax for an accounting period and has not received a notice to file a tax return must give notice of chargeability within 12 months of the end of the accounting period.

The rules on penalties for late notification by taxpayers discussed in Chapter 10 also apply to companies in relation to corporation tax.

COMPANY TAX RETURNS AND KEEPING RECORDS

All companies and organisations must submit their Company Tax Return (Form CT600) online, except in exceptional circumstances. Additionally tax computations and (with very few exceptions) the accounts that form part of the Company Tax Return must be submitted in 'Inline eXtensible Business Reporting Language' (iXBRL) format.

A return for each of the company's accounting periods is due on or before the FILING DUE DATE. This is the normally the **later of**:

(a) **12 months after the end of the period of account concerned**

(b) **Three months from the date on which the notice requiring the return was made**

An obligation to file a return arises only when the company receives a notice requiring a return.

Task 1

Size Ltd prepares accounts for the twelve months to 30 September 2014. A notice requiring a CT600 return for the year ended 30 September 2014 was issued on 1 June 2015. The date by which Size Ltd must file its Company Tax Return for the year to 30 September 2014 is

[   ]

You saw in Chapter six of this Text that if a **period of account** is more than twelve months long, there will be **two accounting periods** based on the period of account. The first accounting period is twelve months long, the second is for the remainder of the period of account.

A tax return must be filed for each accounting period. The tax returns for both accounting periods must be filed within twelve months of the end of the **period of account**.

Task 2

Octo Ltd prepares accounts for the eighteen months to 30 June 2014.

The two accounting periods relating to this period of account are:

[   ]

and

[   ]

The date by which Octo Ltd must file its Company Tax Returns based on this period of account, assuming a notice requiring the returns was issued shortly after the end of the period of account, is:

[   ]

Penalties for late filing

The rules on penalties for late filing of returns as discussed earlier in Chapter 10 of this Text also **apply to companies** in relation to corporation tax.

Task 3

Box Ltd prepares accounts for the twelve months to 31 May 2014. Assume a notice requiring the return for the period was issued shortly after the end of the period of account. Box Ltd filed this return on 24 November 2015. The maximum penalty for late filing is:

£ [   ]

Records

Companies must keep records until the latest of:

(a) **Six years from the end of the accounting period**
(b) The date any enquiries (compliance checks) are completed
(c) The date after which enquiries may not be commenced

All business records and accounts, including contracts and receipts, must be kept.

If a return is demanded more than six years after the end of the accounting period, the company must keep any records that it still has until the later of the end of any enquiry and the expiry of the right to start an enquiry.

Failure to keep records can lead to a penalty of up to £3,000 for each accounting period affected.

Penalties for error

The rules on penalties for errors made by taxpayers discussed in Chapter 10 of this Text **also apply to companies** in relation to Company Tax Returns.

Compliance checks and enquiries

HMRC has the power to conduct a compliance check into a company's tax return in the same way as for an individual's tax return, which was discussed in Chapter 10 this Text.

Remember that an enquiry is a compliance check into a return that has already been filed. Before **HMRC can enquire into a Company Tax Return**, they must give written notice that they are going to enquire **by a year after**:

(a) **The actual filing date** (if the return is filed on or before the due filing date)

(b) **The 31 January, 30 April, 31 July or 31 October next following the actual filing date** (if the return is filed after the due filing date)

Only one enquiry may be made in respect of any one return.

HMRC may demand that the company produce documents. The company may appeal against a notice requiring documents to be produced.

If HMRC demand documents, but the company does not produce them, there is a penalty of £300. There is also a daily penalty of up to £60 per day, which applies for each day from the day after the imposition of the £300 penalty until the documents are produced.

An enquiry ends when HMRC give notice that it has been completed and make any resulting amendments to the return. The company then has 30 days in which it may appeal to the Tax Tribunal against HMRC's amendments.

Task 4

Green Ltd prepares accounts for the twelve months to 30 April 2015. The Company Tax Return for the year was filed on 31 March 2016.

The date by which HMRC may commence an enquiry into the return based on these accounts is:

[   ]

Task 5

A company has been making up its accounts annually to 31 May for many years. For the year ended 31 May 2013, it did not submit its Company Tax Return (CT600) until 1 November 2014. A notice requiring the return was issued on 31 August 2013.

The latest date by which HMRC can commence an enquiry into the company's return is:

[   ]

PAYMENT OF TAX AND INTEREST

All companies and organisations must pay their tax electronically.

Large companies

Large companies must pay their corporation tax in instalments. Broadly, a large company is any company that pays corporation tax at the main rate (profits exceed £1,500,000 for a 12 month accounting period where there are no associated companies).

Instalments are based on the estimated corporation tax liability of the company for the current period (not the previous period). This means that it is extremely important for companies to forecast their tax liabilities accurately. Large companies whose directors are poor at estimating may find their company incurring significant interest charges. The company must estimate its corporation tax liability in time for the first instalment, and must revise its estimate each quarter.

For a 12 month accounting period, **quarterly instalments are due on the 14th day of months 7 and 10 in the accounting period and months 1 and 4 following the end of the period.** You will not be expected to deal with periods other than 12 month periods in your assessment.

HOW IT WORKS

A company which draws up accounts to 31 December 2014 will pay instalments as follows:

Instalment	Due date
1	14 July 2014
2	14 October 2014
3	14 January 2015
4	14 April 2015

Task 6

S Ltd, a large company, has a corporation tax liability of £700,000 in respect of its accounting year 31 March 2015.

Identify which date the company will be required to pay its FINAL instalment of the liability. Tick ONE box.

	✓
14 October 2014	
14 July 2015	
31 July 2015	
1 January 2016	

Interest arises on late paid instalments (from the due date to the actual payment date (see below)). Interest is paid on overpaid instalments, from the actual payment date to the date of repayment, except that interest does not run before the due date for the first instalment. The position is looked at cumulatively after the due date for each instalment.

Exceptions to instalments

If a 'small' company is treated as large as a result of the associated companies rule, it will not have to pay corporation tax by instalments if its own liability is less than £10,000.

If a company is a large company for an accounting period it will not have to pay corporation tax by instalments for that period if:

(a) **Its augmented profits does not exceed £10m** (reduced to reflect any associated companies at the end of the previous period).

(b) **It was not a large company in the previous year**.

Small and medium sized companies

Corporation tax is due for payment nine months and one day after the end of the accounting period by small and medium sized companies.

HOW IT WORKS

K Ltd makes up accounts to 31 March 2015. It is not a large company. The corporation tax for the year to 31 March 2015 is £30,000.

The corporation tax is due on 1 January 2016.

Assessment focus

None of the information in this chapter is included within the 'Taxation Data' which you will be provided with in the live assessment.

The information included in this chapter typically will be tested in the following task:

Task 4 – Taxable total profits and corporation tax payable.

Task 7 – Payments on account and penalties.

Performance feedback

The feedback given below relates to students' performance on the AQ2010 version of the assessments. However, the points made by the assessor will be equally as valid for students sitting the assessment under AQ2013.

Task 2.8 (AQ2010)

Payments dates are also to be expected, but the knowledge expected about instalments is quite basic.

Task 2.9 (AQ2010)

It may be no surprise that this task is the second most poorly performed one in Section 2. Penalties and interest for both individuals and companies is assessable, mainly covering errors and late payment of tax. This is not the exhaustive list, but these areas would be expected in some detail in every question.

CHAPTER OVERVIEW

- A company must usually file its CT600 online return within twelve months of the end of the period of account concerned

- Fixed penalties arise if the return is up to six months late. If the return is over six months late there may be a tax geared penalty

- Companies must normally keep records until six years after the end of the accounting period concerned

- HMRC can enquire into a return. Notice of an enquiry must usually be given within twelve months of the actual filing date

- Large companies must pay their CT liability in 4 instalments starting in the 7th month of the accounting period. The final instalment is due in the fourth month following the end of the accounting period

- Small and medium sized companies must pay their corporation tax liability nine months and one day after the end of an accounting period

Keywords

The **filing due date** – is the date by which a tax return must be filed

Large companies – are companies that pay corporation tax at the main rate

TEST YOUR LEARNING

Test 1

A company has been preparing accounts to 30 June for many years. It submitted its CT600 return for the year to 30 June 2014 on 1 June 2015.

By what date must HMRC give notice that they are going to commence an enquiry into the return?

Test 2

A company filed its CT600 return for the year to 31 December 2014 on 28 February 2016.

What is the maximum penalty in respect of the late filing of the return for the year to 31 December 2014?

£	

Test 3

Girton Ltd has no associated companies. **When will the first payment of corporation tax be due on its taxable profits of £150,000 arising in the year ended 31 December 2014?**

	✓
14 July 2014	
1 October 2015	
31 December 2015	
1 January 2016	

Test 4

Eaton Ltd has taxable total profits of £2,400,000 for its year ended 31 December 2015.

The first instalment of the corporation tax liability for this year will be due on:

	✓
14 April 2015	
14 April 2016	
14 July 2015	
1 October 2016	

Test 5

M Ltd, a large company, has an estimated corporation tax liability of £240,000 in respect of its accounting year 31 March 2015.

What will be the amount of each of the company's quarterly instalments?

£	

chapter 12:
CHARGEABLE GAINS – THE BASICS

chapter coverage 📖

In this chapter we see how to compute chargeable gains or allowable losses arising on the disposal of assets, for both individuals and companies.

We start by considering the rules for individuals. We see how to set allowable losses against chargeable gains and how to arrive at the net gains taxable in any particular tax year. Then we note how to compute the capital gains tax payable in any particular tax year.

Finally we consider the computation of chargeable gains for companies.

The topics covered are:

✍ When does a chargeable gain arise?

✍ Computing chargeable gains and allowable losses for individuals

✍ Computing taxable gains in a tax year

✍ Computing capital gains tax payable

✍ Self assessment for capital gains tax

✍ Computing chargeable gains and allowable losses for companies

INTRODUCTION

We saw earlier in this Text that individuals pay INCOME TAX on all sources of taxable income. This does not however, include gains on the disposal of assets. We will see that an individual needs to do a separate computation for taxable gains and pay CAPITAL GAINS TAX on any gains in the tax year.

In contrast we saw that a company includes net chargeable gains for the accounting period in its corporation tax computation and pays CORPORATION TAX on any gains.

WHEN DOES A CHARGEABLE GAIN ARISE?

For the gain on the disposal of a capital asset to be a chargeable gain there must be a CHARGEABLE DISPOSAL of a CHARGEABLE ASSET by a CHARGEABLE PERSON.

Chargeable persons

Individuals and companies are the only type of chargeable person that you will meet in this Business Tax assessment.

Chargeable disposals

The following are the most important CHARGEABLE DISPOSALS:

- Sales of assets or parts of assets
- Gifts of assets or parts of assets
- The loss or destruction of an asset

A chargeable disposal occurs on the date of the contract (where there is one, whether written or oral), or the date of a conditional contract becoming unconditional.

Exempt disposals include:

- Transfers on death
- Gifts to charities

On death the heirs inherit assets as if they bought them at death for their then market values. There is no capital gain or allowable loss on death.

Chargeable assets

All assets are chargeable assets unless they are specifically designated as exempt.

The following are the **exempt assets** that you need to be aware of:

- Motor vehicles suitable for private use
- Certain chattels (see later in this Chapter)
- Gilt-edged securities (for individuals only)
- Premium bonds (for individuals only)
- Investments held in a NISA (for individuals only)

Any gain arising on the disposal of an exempt asset is not taxable and any loss is not allowable.

Remember that sales of assets as part of the trade of a business (ie sales of inventory) give rise to trading profits and not chargeable gains.

Task 1

Which of the following are chargeable assets for CGT purposes?

	Chargeable ✓	Exempt ✓
A diamond necklace		
A cash sum invested in premium bonds that results in a substantial win		
A vintage Rolls Royce		

COMPUTING CHARGEABLE GAINS AND ALLOWABLE LOSSES FOR INDIVIDUALS

Whenever a **chargeable asset** is disposed of by an individual, a calculation to determine the amount of any gain or loss is needed. The computation follows a standard format as shown below:

	£
Disposal consideration (or market value)	100,000
Less incidental costs of disposal	(1,000)
Net proceeds	99,000
Less allowable costs	(28,000)
Less enhancement expenditure	(1,000)
Chargeable gain	70,000

We now look at each of the items in the above proforma in turn.

We will see later in this chapter that the computation of gains by a company is very similar to that of an individual, however there is an **indexation allowance for a company** but not for an individual.

Disposal consideration

Usually the disposal consideration is the proceeds of sale of the asset, but a disposal is deemed to take place at market value:

    (a)   Where the disposal is by way of a gift

    (b)   Where the disposal is made for a consideration which cannot be valued

    (c)   Where the disposal is made to a connected person (see below)

Costs

The following costs are deducted in the above proforma:

    (a)   **Incidental costs of disposal**

        These are the costs of selling an asset. They may include advertising costs, estate agents' fees, legal costs or valuation fees. These costs should be deducted separately from any other allowable costs.

    (b)   **Allowable costs**

        These include:

        (i)   The original purchase price of the asset

        (ii)   Costs incurred in purchasing the asset (estate agents' fees, legal fees, etc)

    (c)   **Enhancement expenditure**

        This is capital expenditure which enhances the value of the asset and is reflected in the state or nature of the asset at the time of disposal.

Task 2

Jack bought a holiday cottage for £25,000. He paid legal costs of £600 on the purchase.

Jack spent £8,000 building an extension to the cottage.

Jack sold the cottage for £60,000. He paid estate agent's fees of £1,200 and legal costs of £750.

Jack's gain on sale is:

£ [   ]

COMPUTING TAXABLE GAINS IN A TAX YEAR

An individual pays capital gains tax (CGT) on any **taxable gains** arising in a **tax year** (6 April to 5 April).

All the chargeable gains made in the tax year are added together, and any capital losses made in the same tax year are deducted to give net gains (or losses) for the year. Trading losses that can be offset against gains (which we saw in Chapter 8) are deducted next, and then any unrelieved capital losses brought forward from previous years. Finally the annual exempt amount is deducted to arrive at taxable gains, on which capital gains tax will be applied.

A standard format is shown below:

	£
Chargeable gains in tax year	100,000
Less capital losses in tax year	(21,000)
Net gains for the year	79,000
Less trading losses (see Chapter 8)	(6,000)
Less capital losses brought forward	(15,000)
Net chargeable gains	58,000
Less annual exempt amount	(11,000)
Taxable gain	47,000

Annual exempt amount

All individuals (but not companies) are entitled to an annual exempt amount. This may also be referred to as an **annual exemption** in your assessment. For 2014/15 the annual exempt amount is £11,000. As you can see above, it is the last deduction to be made in computing taxable gains, and effectively means that for 2014/15 the first £11,000 of chargeable gains are tax-free for an individual.

Task 3

In 2014/15 Tina has the following gains:

	£
Chargeable gains	18,000

Tina's taxable gains for 2014/15 are:

£ [   ]

Losses

Sometimes an allowable loss rather than a taxable gain arises. Once a loss has been calculated deal with it as follows:

(a) First, set it against gains arising in the same tax year (shown as 'capital losses in tax year' in the above proforma) until these are reduced to £nil, then

(b) Carry any remaining loss forward to set against net gains in the next tax year but only to reduce the net gains in the next tax year down to the level of the annual exempt amount. This means the taxpayer does not lose the benefit of the annual exempt amount. Any loss remaining is carried forward.

HOW IT WORKS

(a) Tim has chargeable gains for 2014/15 of £25,000 and allowable losses of £16,000. As the losses are current year losses they must be fully relieved against the gains to produce net gains of £9,000, despite the fact that net gains are below the annual exempt amount.

	£
Chargeable gains in tax year	25,000
Less losses in tax year	(16,000)
Net chargeable gains	9,000
Less annual exempt amount	(11,000)
Taxable gain	0

(b) Hattie has gains of £11,500 for 2014/15 and allowable losses brought forward of £6,000. Hattie restricts her loss relief to £500 so as to leave net gains of (£11,500 – £500) = £11,000, which will be exactly covered by the annual exempt amount for 2014/15.

	£
Net chargeable gains	11,500
Less losses brought forward	(500)
Less annual exempt amount	(11,000)
Taxable gain	0

The remaining £5,500 of losses will be carried forward to 2015/16.

(c) Mildred has chargeable gains of £2,000 for 2014/15 and losses brought forward from 2013/14 of £12,000. She will not use any loss in 2014/15 but will carry forward all the brought forward losses to 2015/16. The gains of £2,000 are covered by the annual exempt amount for 2014/15.

Task 4

Sally had chargeable gains of £13,000 and allowable losses of £1,000 in 2014/15. She also had allowable losses of £3,000 brought forward from 2013/14.

The capital losses carried forward to 2015/16 are:

	✓
nil	
£4,000	
£3,000	
£2,000	

COMPUTING CAPITAL GAINS TAX PAYABLE

An individual's taxable gains are chargeable to capital gains tax at the rate of 18% or 28% depending on the individual's taxable income for 2014/15. If the individual is a basic rate taxpayer, then CGT is payable at 18% on an amount of taxable gains up to the amount of the taxpayer's unused basic rate band and at 28% on the excess. If the individual is a higher or additional rate taxpayer, then CGT is payable at 28% on all their taxable gains. Note the basic rate band covers taxable income up to £31,865 (for 2014/15), as we saw in Chapter 1.

HOW IT WORKS

(a) Sally has taxable income (ie the amount after the deduction of the personal allowance) of £10,000 in 2014/15 and made taxable gains (ie gains after deduction of the annual exempt amount) of £20,000 in 2014/15.

Sally's capital gains tax liability is:

£20,000 × 18%   £3,600

The taxable income uses £10,000 of the basic rate band, leaving £21,865 of the basic rate band unused, therefore all of the taxable gain is taxed at 18%.

(b) Hector has taxable income of £50,000 in 2014/15 (ie he is a higher rate taxpayer). He made taxable gains of £10,000 in 2014/15.

Hector's capital gains tax liability is:

£10,000 × 28%   £2,800

All of Hector's basic rate band has been taken up by the taxable income, therefore the taxable gain is taxed at 28%.

(c) Isabel has taxable income of £30,000 in 2014/15 and made taxable gains of £25,000 in 2014/15.

Isabel has (£31,865 – £30,000) = £1,865 of her basic rate band unused. Isabel's capital gains tax liability is:

	£
£1,865 × 18%	336
£23,135 × 28%	6,478
£25,000	6,814

Task 5

Sarah made the following chargeable gains and allowable losses in 2014/15.

	£
Gain 17.07.14	21,000
Loss 25.08.14	(4,500)
Gain 15.11.14	17,500

Sarah pays income tax at the additional rate in 2014/15.

The CGT payable for 2014/15 by Sarah is:

£ [   ]

SELF ASSESSMENT FOR CAPITAL GAINS TAX

An individual taxpayer who makes chargeable gains in a tax year is usually required to file details of the gains in a tax return. In many cases, the taxpayer will be filing a tax return for income tax purposes and will include the capital gains supplementary pages. If, however, the taxpayer only has chargeable gains to report, **he must notify his chargeability to HMRC by 5 October following the end of the tax year.** The penalty for late notification is the same as for late notification of income tax chargeability.

The filing date for the tax return is therefore the same as for income tax (as it is part of the self-assessment return) and the same penalties apply for CGT as for income tax in relation to late filing and errors on the return.

Capital gains tax is payable on 31 January following the end of the tax year. There are no payments on account. The consequences of late payment of CGT are the same as for late payment of income tax so penalties and interest may be charged. Repayment interest may be paid on overpayments of CGT.

COMPUTING CHARGEABLE GAINS AND ALLOWABLE LOSSES FOR COMPANIES

Whenever a **chargeable asset** is disposed of by a company, a calculation to determine the amount of any gain or loss is needed. The computation follows a standard format as shown below:

	£
Disposal consideration (or market value)	100,000
Less incidental costs of disposal	(1,000)
Net proceeds	99,000
Less allowable costs	(28,000)
Less enhancement expenditure	(1,000)
Unindexed gain/allowable loss	70,000
Less indexation allowance	(10,000)
Chargeable gain	60,000

You will notice this is very similar to the proforma for an individual with the exception of indexation allowance (see below).

There is also no annual exempt amount for a company. The company's net chargeable gains are calculated, with any brought forward losses being deducted in full. Then instead of deducting the annual exempt amount and charging capital gains tax at 18% or 28% (as for individuals), the gain is added to the company's taxable total profits on which corporation tax is charged (as we saw earlier in this Text).

Indexation allowance

Indexation was introduced to remove the inflationary element of a gain from taxation.

Companies are entitled to an indexation allowance from the date the expenditure was incurred until the date of disposal of the asset.

HOW IT WORKS

M Ltd bought a shop for use in his business on 12 June 1990 and sold it on 1 March 2015.

Indexation allowance is available for the period June 1990 to March 2015.

To calculate an indexation allowance, you need an indexation factor calculated from the month the asset was acquired to the month the asset was sold. You will be given this indexation factor in the assessment. You will not be expected to calculate it.

The indexation factor is multiplied by the cost of the asset (including costs of acquisition) to calculate the indexation allowance.

Similarly, **indexation is available on enhancement expenditure incurred**. This expenditure is multiplied by an indexation factor that runs from the month the expenditure was incurred to the month of sale.

Indexation allowance does not apply to incidental costs of disposal.

HOW IT WORKS

K Ltd bought an asset on 19 August 1994 for £10,000. Enhancement expenditure of £1,000 was incurred on 12 June 2006. The asset was sold for £41,500 on 20 February 2015. The disposal costs were £1,500.

Calculate the chargeable gain arising on the sale of the asset. Indexation factors: August 1994 to February 2015 = 0.804; June 2006 to February 2015 = 0.315.

	£
Disposal consideration	41,500
Less incidental costs of disposal	(1,500)
Net proceeds	40,000
Less purchase price	(10,000)
Less enhancement expenditure	(1,000)
	29,000
Less indexation on purchase price	
£10,000 × 0.804	(8,040)
Less indexation on enhancement expenditure	
£1,000 × 0.315	(315)
Chargeable gain	20,645

Task 6

L Ltd bought a freehold factory in July 2003 for £80,000. It sold the factory for £200,000 in August 2014. The indexation factor from July 2003 – August 2014 = 0.422.

Complete the following computation:

	£
Proceeds	
Cost	
Indexation allowance	
Gain	

The indexation allowance cannot create or increase an allowable loss. If there is a gain before the indexation allowance, the allowance can reduce that gain to zero, but no further. If there is a loss before the indexation allowance, there is no indexation allowance.

Task 7

S plc bought an asset for £50,000 in August 1997 and sold it for £20,000 in January 2015. The indexation factor from August 1997 – January 2015 = 0.637.

The allowable loss is:

£ [ ]

Task 8

T plc bought an asset for £50,000 in August 1997 and sold it for £70,000 in January 2015. The indexation factor from August 1997 – January 2015 = 0.637.

The gain/ loss is:

£ [ ]

Assessment focus

In the live assessment you will be provided with 'Taxation Data' that can be accessed through pop-up windows. The content of these taxation data tables has been reproduced at the front of this Text.

The annual exempt amount and capital gains tax rates within this chapter are included within the taxation data pop-up 1. Make sure you familiarise yourself with the content and practise referring to it as you work through this Text.

The information included in this chapter typically will be tested in the following task:

Task 9 – Basics of capital gains tax

Task 11 – Capital gains tax exemptions, losses, reliefs and tax payable

Performance feedback

The feedback given below relates to students' performance on the AQ2010 version of the assessments. However, the points made by the assessor will be equally as valid for students sitting the assessment under AQ2013.

Task 2.1 (AQ2010)

This is a small task that introduces the topic of capital gains. It mainly covers chargeable persons, assets, disposals and connected persons. It is always a written style question; usually either a multi choice or true/false style.

Over 90% of students met the standard required for competence. This starts the students well for the rest of the tasks in this topic area.

Task 2.2 (AQ2010)

General capital disposals, where students can expect written and computational style questions.

Given that it is quite a straightforward area, the competence demonstrated by students could be better.

Students can expect questions for both individuals and companies, and hence indexation allowances may be included in these questions. Students will never be expected to compute the indexation factor; this will always be provided.

Task 2.4 (AQ2010)

Within this task, students are confused about the order of set off between a capital loss made in the year, a capital loss brought forward and the annual exempt amount.

Task 2.7 (AQ2010)

Basic mistakes are common, such as adding annual exempt amounts instead of deducting and taxing all capital gains at 28% irrespective of the tax status of the individual.

CHAPTER OVERVIEW

- A chargeable gain arises when there is a chargeable disposal of a chargeable asset by a chargeable person

- Enhancement expenditure can be deducted in computing a chargeable gain if it is reflected in the state and nature of the asset at the time of disposal

- Chargeable gains are computed for individuals and companies in a similar way but for companies there is an indexation allowance

- Taxable gains for an individual are net chargeable gains for a tax year (ie minus allowable losses of the current tax year and any unrelieved capital losses brought forward) minus the annual exempt amount

- Losses brought forward by an individual can only reduce net chargeable gains down to the amount of the annual exempt amount

- The rates of CGT are 18% and 28%, but the lower rate of 18% only applies if and to the extent that the individual has any unused basic rate band

- CGT is payable by 31 January following the end of the tax year

- CGT is self assessed and has the same rules about notification of chargeability, penalties and interest as income tax

- The indexation allowance gives relief for the inflation element of a gain for a company

Keywords

Chargeable person – an individual or company

Chargeable asset – any asset that is not an exempt asset

Chargeable disposal – a sale or gift of an asset

Exempt disposal – a disposal on which no chargeable gain or allowable loss arises

Enhancement expenditure – capital expenditure that enhances the value of the asset and is reflected in the state or nature of the asset at the time of disposal

Taxable gains – the chargeable gains of an individual for a tax year, after deducting allowable losses of the same tax year, any unrelieved capital losses brought forward and the annual exempt amount

BPP
LEARNING MEDIA

TEST YOUR LEARNING

Test 1

Tick to show if the following disposals would be chargeable or exempt for CGT?

	Chargeable ✓	Exempt ✓
A gift of an antique necklace		
The sale of a building		

Test 2

Yvette buys an investment property for £325,000. She sells the property on 12 December 2014 for £560,000.

Her chargeable gain on sale is:

£

Test 3

Philip has chargeable gains of £171,000 and allowable losses of £5,300 in 2014/15. Losses brought forward at 6 April 2014 amount to £10,000.

The amount liable to CGT in 2014/15 is:

£

The losses carried forward are:

£

Test 4

Martha is a higher rate taxpayer who made chargeable gains (before the annual exempt amount) of £23,900 in October 2014.

Martha's CGT liability for 2014/15 is:

£

Test 5

The payment date for capital gains tax for 2014/15 is (insert date as XX/XX/XX):

Test 6

Indexation allowance runs from [   ] to [   ].

Fill in the blanks with words of explanation.

Test 7

J plc bought a plot of land in July 2005 for £80,000. It spent £10,000 on drainage in April 2008. It sold the land for £200,000 in August 2014. The indexation factors from July 2005 – August 2014 = 0.341 and from April 2008 – August 2014 = 0.205.

Using the proforma layout provided, compute the gain on sale.

	£
Proceeds of sale	
Less cost	
Less enhancement expenditure	
Less indexation allowance on cost	
Less indexation allowance on enhancement	
Chargeable gain	

chapter 13:
FURTHER ASPECTS OF CHARGEABLE GAINS

chapter coverage 📖

In the previous chapter we learnt the basics of computing chargeable gains for individuals and companies. In this chapter we look at how to deal with certain specific types of disposal.

We start by considering how to compute chargeable gains and allowable losses on part disposals and chattels, and how they apply to both individuals and companies.

We then look at some special rules for individuals when dealing with disposals to connected persons and spouses or civil partners.

The topics that we shall cover are:

✍ Part disposals

✍ Chattels

✍ Connected persons for individuals

✍ Spouses/civil partners

PART DISPOSALS

Sometimes part, rather than the whole of an asset is disposed of. For instance, one-third of a piece of land may be sold. In this case, we need to be able to compute the chargeable gain or allowable loss arising on the part of the asset disposed of.

The problem is that although we know what the disposal proceeds are for the part of the asset disposed of, we do not usually know what proportion of the 'cost' of the whole asset relates to that part. The solution to this is to **use the following fraction to determine the cost of the part disposed of.**

The fraction is:

$$\frac{A}{A+B} = \frac{\text{Value of the part disposed of}}{\text{Value of the part disposed of} + \text{Market value of the remainder}}$$

A is the 'gross' proceeds (or market value) before deducting incidental costs of disposal.

You must learn the above formula for use in your assessment.

The formula is used to apportion the cost of the whole asset. If, however, any expenditure was incurred wholly in respect of the part disposed of, it should be treated as an allowable deduction in full for that part and not apportioned. An example of this is incidental selling expenses, which are wholly attributable to the part disposed of.

HOW IT WORKS

Mr Jones bought four acres of land for £270,000. He sold one acre of the land at auction for £200,000, before auction expenses of 15%. The market value of the three remaining acres is £460,000.

The cost of the land being sold is:

$$\frac{200,000}{200,000 + 460,000} \times £270,000 = £81,818$$

	£
Disposal proceeds	200,000
Less incidental costs of sale (15% × £200,000)	(30,000)
Net proceeds	170,000
Less cost (see above)	(81,818)
Chargeable gain	88,182

Task 1

Yarrek bought a plot of land for investment purposes for £100,000. In January 2015, he sold part of the land for £391,000, which was net of legal fees on the sale of £9,000. At that time, the value of the remaining land was £600,000.

The chargeable gain arising on the disposal is:

£ [   ]

CHATTELS

A CHATTEL is **tangible moveable property** (ie property that can be moved, seen and touched). Examples are items such as furniture and works of art.

A WASTING CHATTEL is a **chattel with an estimated remaining useful life of 50 years or less.** An example would be a racehorse or a greyhound. **Wasting chattels are exempt assets** (so that there are no chargeable gains and no allowable losses). There is one exception to this, being plant and machinery used in the taxpayer's trade, but this will not be tested in your assessment. So for the purpose of your assessment wasting chattels are exempt.

Task 2

Jackson bought a racing greyhound for £6,000. The greyhound was sold for £10,000.

Decide whether the following statement is True or False.

A chargeable gain of £4,000 arises on the disposal.

	✓
True	
False	

There are special rules for calculating gains and losses on non-wasting chattels:

(a) If a chattel is not a wasting asset, any gain arising on its disposal will still be exempt from CGT if the asset is sold for gross proceeds of £6,000 or less.

(b) If sale proceeds exceed £6,000, but the cost is less than £6,000 the gain is limited to:

5/3 × (gross proceeds – £6,000)

(c) If sale proceeds are less than £6,000, any allowable loss is restricted to that which would arise if it were sold for gross proceeds of £6,000

We will look at examples of each of these situations in turn.

HOW IT WORKS

John purchased a painting for £3,000. On 1 January 2015 he sold the painting at auction.

If the gross sale proceeds are £4,000, the gain on sale will be exempt.

If the gross sale proceeds are £8,000 with costs of sale of 10%, the gain arising on the disposal of the painting will be calculated as follows:

	£
Gross proceeds	8,000
Less incidental costs of sale (10% × £8,000)	(800)
Net proceeds	7,200
Less cost	(3,000)
Chargeable gain	4,200
Gain cannot exceed 5/3 × £(8,000 – 6,000)	£3,333

Therefore chargeable gain is £3,333.

Task 3

Jacky purchased a non-wasting chattel for £2,500. On 1 October 2014 she sold the chattel at auction for gross proceeds of £10,000 (which was subject to auctioneer's commission of 5%). The gain arising is:

	✓
nil	
£5,833	
£7,000	
£6,667	

HOW IT WORKS

Magee purchased an antique desk for £8,000. She sold the desk in an auction for £4,750 net of auctioneer's fees of 5% in November 2014.

Magee obviously has a loss and therefore the allowable loss is calculated on **deemed proceeds of £6,000.** The costs of disposal can be deducted from the deemed proceeds of £6,000.

	£
Deemed disposal proceeds	6,000
Less incidental costs of disposal (£4,750 × 5/95)	(250)
	5,750
Less cost	(8,000)
Allowable loss	(2,250)

Task 4

Jameel purchased a non-wasting chattel for £8,800 which he sold at auction for £3,600 (which was net of 10% commission).

The allowable loss is: (both minus signs and brackets can be used to indicate negative numbers):

£ [   ]

Interaction of chattels and part disposals

When the part disposal rules are applied to the sale of 'part of an asset', the allocation of the cost between the part disposed of and the remaining asset may then result in the need to consider the chattels rules. The rules only apply to chattels and not, for example, the part disposal of land (which is not tangible moveable property).

HOW IT WORKS

Miguel owned three vases. He had bought these together for £7,500. He sold one of the vases in October 2014 for £9,000. The other two vases were worth £13,500 at that time. As we know, this is treated as a part disposal of the set.

The gain on sale of one vase

	£
Proceeds	9,000
Less cost (9,000/(9,000 + 13,500)) × £7,500	(3,000)
Gain	6,000

As the apportioned cost is now < £6,000 the chattel rules will be applied:

Gain cannot exceed 5/3 × £(9,000 − 6,000)	5,000

Note. There are special rules that prevent taxpayers splitting up a set of assets and selling them separately in order to use the £6,000 exemption, but these rules are not in your syllabus.

Task 5

In 2014/15, Mr California sold the following chattels.

Chattel	Cost	Proceeds
	£	£
Vase	800	7,000
Sideboard	7,000	5,000

All proceeds are shown before deducting selling expenses of 5% of the gross proceeds. Compute the chargeable gain or allowable loss on each chattel.

Chattels and part disposals for companies

The rules relating to chattels and part disposals also apply to disposals by companies, but with indexation allowances applied to the allowable costs. Note that with part disposals, the indexation allowance is multiplied by the apportioned cost of the part of the asset being disposed of.

HOW IT WORKS

We will use the same example as earlier in this chapter but change Mr Jones to Jones Ltd.

Jones Ltd bought four acres of land for £270,000 to hold as an investment. It sold one acre of the land at auction for £200,000, before auction expenses of 15%. The market value of the three remaining acres is £460,000. Assume the indexation factor applicable is 0.850.

The cost of the land being sold is:

$$\frac{200{,}000}{200{,}000 + 460{,}000} \times £270{,}000 = £81{,}818$$

	£
Disposal proceeds	200,000
Less incidental costs of sale (15%)	(30,000)
Net proceeds	170,000
Less cost (see above)	(81,818)
	88,182
Less indexation allowance £81,818 × 0.850	(69,545)
Chargeable gain	18,637

Task 6

Y Ltd bought a set of four paintings for investment purposes for £120,000 in June 2005. In January 2015, it sold one painting for gross proceeds of £100,000, and incurred legal fees on the sale of £8,000. At that time, the value of the remaining three paintings was £255,000. The indexation factor between June 2005 and January 2015 is 0.350.

(1)   The cost of the painting sold is:

£ [   ]

(2)   The chargeable gain arising on the disposal is:

£ [   ]

CONNECTED PERSONS FOR INDIVIDUALS

If a disposal by an individual is made to a connected person, **the disposal is deemed to take place at the market value of the asset.**

If an **allowable loss arises** on the disposal, it can **only be set against gains** arising in the same or future tax years from disposals **to the same connected person**, and the loss can only be set off if he or she is still connected with the person making the loss.

For this purpose an individual is connected with:

- His relatives (brothers, sisters, lineal ancestors and lineal descendants)
- The relatives of his spouse/civil partner
- The spouses/civil partners of his and his spouse's/civil partner's relatives

Task 7

On 1 August 2014 Holly sold a painting to her sister, Emily for £40,000. The market value of the painting on the date of sale was £50,000. Holly had bought the painting for £60,000.

The allowable loss arising on disposal of the painting by Holly is (both minus signs and brackets can be used to indicate negative numbers):

£ [   ]

Explain how may this be relieved.

SPOUSES/CIVIL PARTNERS

Spouses/civil partners are taxed as two separate people. Each individual has an annual exempt amount, and allowable losses of one individual cannot be set against gains of the other.

Disposals between spouses/civil partners do not give rise to chargeable gains or allowable losses. The disposal is said to be on a 'NO GAIN/NO LOSS' basis. The acquiring spouse/civil partner takes the base cost of the disposing spouse/civil partner.

Task 8

William sold an asset to his wife Kate in May 2014 for £32,000 when its market value was £45,000. William acquired the asset for £14,000 in June 2004.

Calculate the chargeable gain on this transfer. Tick ONE box

	✓
nil	
£18,000	
£31,000	
£13,000	

Assessment focus

None of the information in this chapter is included within the 'Taxation Data' available in the live assessment.

The information included in this chapter typically will be tested in the following task:

Task 9 – Basics of capital gains tax

Performance feedback

The feedback given below relates to students' performance on the AQ2010 version of the assessments. However, the points made by the assessor will be equally as valid for students sitting the assessment under AQ2013.

Task 2.1 (AQ2010)

This is a small task that introduces the topic of capital gains. It mainly covers chargeable persons, assets, disposals and connected persons. It is always a written style question; usually either a multi choice or true/false style.

Over 90% of students met the standard required for competence. This starts the students well for the rest of the tasks in this topic area.

Task 2.2 (AQ2010)

Capital disposals - gains and losses

General capital disposals, including chattels and part disposals, are incorporated into this task. Students can expect written and computational style questions.

Given that it is quite a straightforward area, the competence demonstrated by students could be better. Part disposals clearly cause the most problems, with many students faced with this topic gaining no marks at all. Although chattels are reasonably well handled, there are students who have shown the chattel formula as Proceeds – Cost × 3/5, instead of Proceeds – 6,000 × 5/3. This is quite basic knowledge and shows a lack of robust preparation for the assessment.

Students can expect questions for both individuals and companies, and hence indexation allowances may be included in these questions. Students will never be expected to compute the indexation factor; this will always be provided.

CHAPTER OVERVIEW

- On the part disposal of an asset the formula A/(A + B) must be applied to work out the cost attributable to the part disposed of

- Wasting chattels are exempt assets (eg racehorses and greyhounds)

- If a non-wasting chattel is sold for gross proceeds of £6,000 or less, any gain arising is exempt.

- If gross proceeds exceed £6,000 on the sale of a non-wasting chattel but the cost is less than £6,000, any gain arising on the disposal of the asset is limited to 5/3 × (Gross proceeds – £6,000)

- If the gross proceeds are less than £6,000 on the sale of a non-wasting chattel, any loss otherwise arising is restricted by deeming the gross proceeds to be £6,000

- A disposal to a connected person takes place at market value

- For individuals, connected people are broadly brothers, sisters, lineal ancestors and descendants and their spouses/civil partners plus similar relations of a spouse/civil partner

- Losses on disposals to connected people can only be set against gains on disposals to the same connected person

- Disposals between spouses/civil partners take place on a no gain/no loss basis

Keywords

Part disposal – When part, rather than a whole asset is disposed of.

Chattel – tangible moveable property

Wasting chattel – a chattel with an estimated remaining useful life of 50 years or less

TEST YOUR LEARNING

Test 1

Tick to show the correct answer.

Richard sells four acres of land (out of a plot of ten acres) for £38,000 in July 2014. Costs of disposal amount to £3,000. The ten-acre plot cost £41,500. The market value of the six acres remaining is £48,000.

The chargeable gain/allowable loss arising is:

	✓
£16,663	
£17,500	
£19,663	
£18,337	

Test 2

Mustafa bought a non-wasting chattel for £3,500.

The gain arising if he sells it for:

(a) **£5,800 after deducting selling expenses of £180 is:**

£ _____

(b) **£8,200 after deducting selling expenses of £220 is:**

£ _____

Test 3

Simon bought a racehorse for £4,500. He sold the racehorse for £9,000 in December 2014.

The gain arising is:

£ _____

Test 4

Santa bought a painting for £7,000. He sold the painting in June 2014 for £5,000.

The loss arising is: (both minus signs and brackets can be used to indicate negative numbers):

£ _____

Test 5

X Ltd bought four acres of land for £50,000 in December 2009. In February 2015, it sold one acre of the land for £80,000. At the time of the sale, the value of the three remaining acres was £120,000. The indexation factor between December 2009 and February 2015 is 0.198.

(1) **The cost of the part of the land sold is:**

£ _____

(2) **The chargeable gain arising on the disposal is:**

£ _____

Test 6

M plc purchased a non-wasting chattel for £3,500 in August 2012. In October 2014 it sold the chattel at auction for £8,000. The indexation factor between August 2012 and October 2014 is 0.065.

The gain arising is:

£ _____

Test 7

S Ltd bought a non-wasting chattel for £8,700 in October 2008. It sold the chattel for £4,300 in May 2014. The indexation factor between October 2008 and May 2014 is 0.175.

Calculate the allowable loss on sale. Tick ONE box.

	✓
£(5,923)	
£(4,400)	
£(2,700)	
£(4,223)	

Test 8

Decide whether the following statement is True or False.

A loss arising on a disposal to a connected person can be set against any gains arising in the same tax year or in subsequent tax years.

	✓
True	
False	

Test 9

Decide whether the following statement is True or False.

No gain or loss arises on a disposal to a spouse/civil partner.

	✓
True	
False	

Test 10

Complete the table by ticking the appropriate box for each scenario.

	Actual proceeds used	Deemed proceeds (market value) used	No gain or loss basis
Paul sells an asset to his civil partner Joe for £3,600			
Grandmother gives an asset to her grandchild worth £1,000			
Sarah sells an asset to best friend Cathy for £12,000 worth £20,000			

chapter 14:
SHARE DISPOSALS

———— chapter coverage 📖 ————

In this chapter we see how to compute chargeable gains and allowable losses on the disposal of shares for both individuals and companies.

This is a very important chapter as the computation of gains and losses on the disposal of shares is a key task in your assessment. You will not be provided with a structured proforma for these tasks in the assessment and these will be humanly marked. Therefore, you will need to be prepared to set out a computation in the way outlined in this chapter.

The topics covered are:

✍ Why special rules are needed for shares

✍ Matching rules for individuals

✍ Share pool

✍ Bonus and rights issues for individuals

✍ Matching rules for companies

✍ The FA 1985 pool

✍ Bonus issues and rights issues for companies

WHY SPECIAL RULES ARE NEEDED FOR SHARES

Shares present special problems when computing gains or losses on disposal. For instance, suppose that a taxpayer buys some shares in X plc on the following dates:

	No of shares	Cost
		£
5 July 1992	150	195
17 January 1997	100	375
2 July 2014	100	1,000

On 15 June 2014, he sells 220 of his shares for £3,300. **To work out his chargeable gain, we need to be able to identify which shares** out of his three holdings **were actually sold**. Since one share is identical to any other, it is not possible to work this out by reference to factual evidence.

As a result, it has been necessary to devise 'matching rules'. These allow us to identify on a disposal which shares have been sold and so **work out what the allowable cost** (and therefore the gain) **on disposal should be.** These matching rules are considered in detail below.

It is very important that you understand the matching rules. These rules are very regularly assessed and if you do not understand them you will not be able to get any of this part of a task right.

MATCHING RULES FOR INDIVIDUALS

For individuals the matching of the shares sold is in the following order:

(a) **Shares acquired on the same day**

(b) **Shares acquired in the following thirty days** on a FIFO (first in, first out) basis

(c) **Shares from the share pool**. The share pool includes all other shares not acquired on the dates above, and is explained below

Task 1

Noah acquired shares in Ark Ltd as follows.

2 August 2011	10,000 shares
25 April 2013	10,000 shares
17 June 2014	1,000 shares
19 June 2014	2,000 shares

Noah sold 15,000 shares on 17 June 2014.

Which shares is he selling for capital gains tax purposes?

SHARE POOL

The share pool includes shares acquired up to the day before the disposal on which we are calculating the gain or loss. It grows when an acquisition is made and shrinks when a disposal is made.

The calculation of the share pool value

To compute the value of the share pool, set-up two columns of figures:

(a)   The number of shares
(b)   The cost of the shares

Each time shares are acquired, both the number and the cost of the acquired shares are added to those already in the pool.

When there is a disposal from the pool, both the number of shares being disposed of, and a cost relating to those shares, are deducted from the pool. The cost of the disposal is calculated as a proportion of total cost in the pool, based on the number of shares being sold.

HOW IT WORKS

Jackie bought 10,000 shares in X plc for £6,000 in August 1995 and another 10,000 shares for £9,000 in December 2007.

She sold 12,000 shares for £24,000 in August 2014.

The share pool is:

	No of shares	Cost £
August 1995 Acquisition	10,000	6,000
December 2007 Acquisition	10,000	9,000
	20,000	15,000
August 2014 Disposal	(12,000)	(9,000)
(£15,000 ×12,000/20,000 = £9,000)		
c/f	8,000	6,000

The gain is:

	£
Proceeds of sale	24,000
Less allowable cost	(9,000)
Chargeable gain	15,000

Task 2

Joraver bought 9,000 shares in Z plc for £4,500 in May 1999. He sold 2,000 shares in August 2008 for £3,500. He then bought a further 5,000 shares for £7,500 in May 2011.

Joraver sold 10,000 shares for £20,000 in January 2015.

The gain on the sale in 2015 is:

£	

HOW IT WORKS

Tony bought shares in A Ltd as follows.

11 May 2004	14,000 shares for £20,000
9 April 2009	5,000 shares for £12,000
15 June 2014	5,000 shares for £15,000

He sold 18,000 shares for £49,500 on 5 June 2014.

The disposal is matched first against the acquisition in the next 30 days and then against the shares in the share pool as follows.

1 Sale of 5,000 shares bought on 15 June 2014
2 Sale of 13,000 shares from the share pool

Disposal of 5,000 shares bought on 15 June 2014

	£
Proceeds of sale $\dfrac{5,000}{18,000} \times £49,500$	13,750
Less allowable cost	(15,000)
Allowable loss	(1,250)

Disposal of 13,000 shares from the share pool

	£
Proceeds of sale $\dfrac{13,000}{18,000} \times £49,500$	35,750
Less allowable cost (W)	(21,895)
Chargeable gain	13,855

Therefore the net chargeable gain is:

£(13,855 – 1,250)	12,605

Working	No of shares	Cost
		£
11 May 2004 Acquisition	14,000	20,000
9 April 2009 Acquisition	5,000	12,000
	19,000	32,000
5 June 2014 Disposal	(13,000)	(21,895)
(£32,000 × 13,000/19,000 = £21,895)		
c/f	6,000	10,105

Task 3

Eliot acquired shares in K Ltd as follows.

10 August 2006	5,000 shares for £10,000
15 April 2009	2,000 shares for £5,000
25 July 2014	1,000 shares for £3,800
27 July 2014	500 shares for £1,700

Eliot sold 6,000 shares for £21,600 on 25 July 2014.

Calculate the net chargeable gain arising on the disposal by Eliot.

BONUS AND RIGHTS ISSUES FOR INDIVIDUALS

Bonus issues

BONUS SHARES are **additional shares given free to shareholders based on their current holding(s).** For example, a shareholder may own 2,000 shares. The company makes a 1 share for every 2 shares held bonus issue (called 1 for 2 bonus issue). The shareholder will then have an extra 1,000 shares, giving him 3,000 shares overall.

Sometimes this is done when shares become quite expensive and so less easy to trade. For example, where a share in a company is worth £20, it might be better from a trading point of view to have 4 shares worth £5 each. The company could issue 3 bonus shares for each one share owned (a 3 for 1 bonus issue). The overall value of each shareholder's holding will not change as a result of the bonus issue but the value of each share will be reduced. **Bonus shares are treated as being acquired at the date of the original acquisition of the underlying shares giving rise to the bonus issue.**

Since bonus shares are issued at no cost there is **no need to adjust the original cost.**

Rights issues

In a RIGHTS ISSUE, a **shareholder is offered the right to buy additional shares by the company in proportion to the shares he already holds.**

A company may do this if it wants to raise extra capital. The rights shares may be offered at a discount to the market value to encourage shareholders to take up the offer rather than buying shares from other shareholders as this does not benefit the company. The difference between a bonus issue and a rights issue is that in a rights issue the new shares are paid for. This results in an **adjustment to the original cost.**

HOW IT WORKS

Jonah acquired 20,000 shares for £34,200 in T plc in April 2004. There was a 1 for 2 bonus issue in May 2009 and a 1 for 5 rights issue in August 2014 at £1.20 per share.

Jonah sold 30,000 shares for £45,000 in December 2014.

The share pool is constructed as follows:

	No of shares	Cost £
April 2004 Acquisition	20,000	34,200
May 2009 Bonus 1 for 2 (1/2 × 20,000 = 10,000)	10,000	–
	30,000	34,200
August 2014 Rights 1 for 5 @ £1.20	6,000	7,200
(1/5 × 30,000 = 6,000 shares × £1.20 = £7,200)		
	36,000	41,400
December 2014 Disposal	(30,000)	(34,500)
(£41,400 × 30,000/36,000 = £34,500)		
c/f	6,000	6,900

The gain on sale is:

	£
Proceeds of sale	45,000
Less allowable cost	(34,500)
Chargeable gain	10,500

Task 4

Dorothy bought 2,000 shares for £10,000 in S Ltd in August 2004. There was a 1 for 1 rights issue at £2.50 in May 2007 and Dorothy took up all her rights issue shares. There was a 1 for 4 bonus issue in September 2010.

Dorothy sold 3,000 shares for £18,000 in October 2014. Her chargeable gain on sale is:

£ [   ]

MATCHING RULES FOR COMPANIES

For companies the matching of shares sold is in the following order.

    (a) **Shares acquired on the same day**.

    (b) **Shares acquired in the previous nine days** (if more than one acquisition, on a 'first in, first out' basis – FIFO).

    (c) **Shares from the FA 1985 pool** which is a pool of other share acquisitions.

The composition of the FA 1985 pool is explained in more detail below.

There is no indexation allowance on shares acquired in the previous nine days, even if the acquisition is in the previous month to the disposal.

HOW IT WORKS

Z Ltd acquired the following shares in L plc:

Date of acquisition	No of shares
9 November 2006	15,000
15 December 2008	15,000
11 July 2014	5,000
15 July 2014	5,000

Z Ltd disposed of 20,000 of the shares on 15 July 2014.

We match the 20,000 shares sold to acquisitions as follows.

(a) Acquisition on same day: 5,000 shares acquired 15 July 2014.

(b) Acquisitions in previous 9 days: 5,000 shares acquired 11 July 2014.

(c) FA 1985 share pool: 10,000 shares out of 30,000 shares in FA 1985 share pool (9 November 2006 and 15 December 2008).

Task 5

B Ltd acquired shares in J plc as follows:

Date of acquisition	No. of shares
9 October 2008	1,000
11 June 2010	1,500
12 July 2014	1,200

B Ltd sold 2,000 of the shares on 15 July 2014.

Decide how the shares disposed of will be matched. Tick ONE box.

	✓
1,000 shares acquired on 9 October 2008, then with 1,000 shares acquired on 11 June 2010	
2,000 shares from the acquisitions in 2008 and 2010 in the FA 1985 pool	
2,000 shares from the acquisitions in 2008, 2010 and 2014 in the FA 1985 pool	
1,200 shares acquired on 12 July 2014, then with 800 shares in the FA 1985 pool	

THE FA 1985 POOL

The FA 1985 pool comprises the following shares:

(a) Shares held by a company on 1 April 1985 and acquired by that company on or after 1 April 1982.

(b) Shares acquired by that company on or after 1 April 1985.

We must keep track of:

(a) The number of shares
(b) The cost of the shares ignoring indexation
(c) The indexed cost of the shares

For historical reasons, your first step with a FA 1985 pool should be to compute its **value at 1 April 1985.** To do this **aggregate the indexed cost and number of shares acquired between April 1982 and 1 April 1985.** In order to calculate the indexed cost of these shares, an indexation allowance, computed from the date of acquisition of the shares to April 1985, is added to the cost value.

HOW IT WORKS

J Ltd bought 10,000 shares in X plc for £6,000 in August 1982 and another 10,000 for £9,000 in December 1984. Assume indexation factors between August 1982 – April 1985 = 0.157 and December 1984 – April 1985 = 0.043.

Compute the value of the FA 1985 pool at 1 April 1985.

	No of shares	Cost £	Indexed cost £
August 1982 (a)	10,000	6,000	6,000
December 1984 (b)	10,000	9,000	9,000
	20,000	15,000	15,000
Index to April 1985			
£6,000 × 0.157 (a)			942
£9,000 × 0.043 (b)			387
Pool at 5 April 1985	20,000	15,000	16,329

Your second step should be to reflect all disposals and acquisitions of shares in the FA 1985 pool between **1 April 1985 and ten days before the disposal.** Disposals/acquisitions of shares that decrease/increase the amount of expenditure within the FA 1985 pool are called OPERATIVE EVENTS.

You must reflect each operative event in the FA 1985 pool. However, prior to reflecting an operative event within the FA 1985 share pool, a further indexation allowance (sometimes described as an indexed rise) must be computed up to the date of the operative event you are looking at. You must look at each operative event in chronological order.

HOW IT WORKS

Following on from the above example, now assume that J Ltd acquired 4,000 more shares on 1 January 1990 at a cost of £6,000.

Show the value of the FA 1985 pool on 1 January 1990 following the acquisition. The indexation factor April 1985 – January 1990 = 0.261.

	No of shares	Cost £	Indexed cost £
1 April 1985	20,000	15,000	16,329
Index to January 1990			
0.261 × £16,329			4,262
			20,591
January 1990 acquisition	4,000	6,000	6,000
	24,000	21,000	26,591

If there are several operative events, the procedure described must be performed several times over. In the case of a disposal, following the calculation of the indexed rise, the cost and the indexed cost attributable to the shares disposed of are deducted from the cost and the indexed cost columns within the FA 1985 pool. This is computed on a pro-rata basis if only part of the holding is being sold.

HOW IT WORKS

Continuing the above example, suppose that J Ltd now disposes of 12,000 shares on 9 January 2015 for £26,000.

Show the value of the FA 1985 pool on 10 January 2015 following the disposal. Compute the gain on the disposal. The indexation factor January 1990 – January 2015 = 1.171.

	No of shares	Cost £	Indexed cost £
Value at January 1990	24,000	21,000	26,591
Indexed rise to January 2015 1.171 × £26,591			31,138
	24,000	21,000	57,729
Disposal (×12,000/24,000)	(12,000)	(10,500)	(28,865)
Pool c/f	12,000	10,500	28,864

The gain on the disposal is calculated as follows:

	£
Sale proceeds	26,000
Less cost	(10,500)
	15,500
Less indexation (£28,865 – £10,500)	(18,365)
Gain	nil

Note that the indexation for the shares sold is the difference between the indexed cost and the cost, and that the indexation cannot create a loss.

Task 6

W Ltd acquired and disposed of shares in Z plc as follows:

No of shares	Date	Cost £
3,000	10 August 2005	9,000
10,000	25 April 2007	45,000
(1,000)	13 September 2010	–
(8,500)	24 November 2014	–

The proceeds of sale of the shares sold on 24 November 2014 were £47,200.

(1) Using the proforma layout provided, show the share pool of Z plc shares. Indexation factors are as follows:

August 2005 – April 2007	0.066
April 2007 – September 2010	0.097
September 2010 – November 2014	0.149

	No of shares	Cost £	Indexed cost £

(2) Calculate the gain on sale in November 2014.

	£
Proceeds	
Less cost	
Less indexation allowance	
Chargeable gain	

BONUS ISSUES AND RIGHTS ISSUES FOR COMPANIES

Bonus issue

As we saw earlier in this chapter A BONUS ISSUE is where **additional shares are given free to shareholders based on their current holdings.** Since bonus shares are issued at no cost there is no need to adjust the original costs. Instead the number of shares purchased at particular times are increased by the bonus issue. **There is no need to index the FA 1985 pool to the date of the bonus issue as this is not classed as an 'operative event'.** The normal matching rules apply.

Rights issue

A RIGHTS ISSUE is where shareholders in a company are **offered the right to buy new shares in that company based on their current holdings.** Rights shares are treated as being acquired at the date of the original acquisition of the underlying shares giving rise to the rights issue. Therefore, rights shares derived from shares in the FA 1985 pool go into that holding. You should add the number and cost of each rights issue to each holding as appropriate. This is important to remember if you are looking at rights issue shares acquired and then disposed of within nine days. The nine day rule will not apply to these shares as they will be treated for matching purposes as having been acquired on the original date of acquisition of the underlying shares.

However, for the purposes of calculating the indexation allowance for rights issues, expenditure on a rights issue is taken as being incurred on the date of the issue and not on the acquisition date of the original holding. Therefore **the FA 1985 pool needs to be indexed to the date of the rights issue as this is classed as an 'operative event'.**

HOW IT WORKS

S Ltd had the following transactions in the shares of B Ltd

May 1989	Purchased 2,000 shares for £4,000
May 2003	Took up one for two rights issue at £2.00 per share
October 2014	Sold all the shares for £14,000

Compute the chargeable gain or allowable loss arising on the sale in October 2013.

Indexation factors:

May 1989 – May 2003 = 0.578

May 2003 – October 2014 = 0.425

	No of shares	Cost £	Indexed cost £
May 1989	2,000	4,000	4,000
Indexed rise to May 2003			
£4,000 × 0.578			2,312
			6,312
Rights issue 1 for 2 (1/2 × 2,000)	1,000	2,000	2,000
	3,000	6,000	8,312
Indexed rise to October 2014			
£8,312 × 0.425			3,533
	3,000	6,000	11,845

	£
Disposal proceeds	14,000
Less cost	(6,000)
Less indexation (£11,845 – £6,000)	(5,845)
Chargeable gain	2,155

Task 7

S Ltd bought 10,000 shares in T plc in May 2003 at a cost of £45,000.

There was a 2 for 1 bonus issue in October 2005.

There was a 1 for 3 rights issue in June 2009 at a cost of £4 per share. S Ltd took up all of its rights entitlement.

S Ltd sold 20,000 shares in T plc for £120,000 in January 2015.

The indexed rise between May 2003 and June 2009 is 0.176 and between June 2009 and January 2015 is 0.216.

(1)   Using the pro forma layout provided, show the share pool.

	No of shares	Cost £	Indexed cost £

(2)   The gain on sale is:

£ [   ]

Assessment focus

None of the information in this chapter is included within the 'Taxation Data' available in the live assessment.

The information included in this chapter typically will be tested in the following task:

Task 10 – Taxation of shares – This task is humanly marked.

Performance feedback

The feedback given below relates to students' performance on the AQ2010 version of the assessments. However, the points made by the assessor will be equally as valid for students sitting the assessment under AQ2013.

Task 2.3 (AQ2010)

This is a humanly marked task that covers the disposal of shares. Students can expect all aspects of shares, including bonus issues, rights issues, matching rules for both individuals and limited companies. It is reasonably well handled by most students, with the problems arising, as might be expected, with the matching rules.

Such a problem is not that the student does not know the matching rules, but that the student does not read the dates carefully enough to accurately apply those matching rules.

CHAPTER OVERVIEW

- The matching rules for individuals are:

  - Same day acquisitions
  - Next 30 days acquisitions on a FIFO basis
  - Shares in the share pool

- The share pool runs up to the day before disposal

- Bonus issue and rights issue shares are acquired in proportion to the shareholder's existing holding

- The difference between a bonus and a rights issue is that in a rights issue shares are paid for

- The matching rules for companies are:

  - Same day acquisitions
  - Previous 9 days acquisitions on a FIFO basis
  - Shares in the FA 1985 share pool

- In the FA 1985 share pool, we must keep track of the number of shares, the cost of the shares and the indexed cost

- Operative events increase or decrease the amount of expenditure within the FA 1985 pool

- For a company a rights issue is treated as an operative event, whereas a bonus issue is not

Keywords

Bonus shares – shares that are issued free to shareholders based on original holdings

Rights issues – similar to bonus issues except that in a rights issue shares must be paid for

Operative events – are disposals/acquisitions of shares that decrease/ increase the amount of expenditure within the FA 1985 pool

TEST YOUR LEARNING

Test 1

Tasha bought 10,000 shares in V plc in August 1993 for £5,000 and a further 10,000 shares for £16,000 in April 2008. She sold 15,000 shares for £30,000 in November 2014.

Tick to show what her chargeable gain is.

	✓
£15,750	
£11,500	
£17,000	
£14,250	

Test 2

Tick to show whether the following statement is True or False.

In both a bonus issue and a rights issue, there is an adjustment to the original cost of the shares.

	✓
True	
False	

Test 3

Marcus bought 2,000 shares in X plc in May 2002 for £12,000. There was a 1 for 2 rights issue at £7.50 per share in December 2003. Marcus sold 2,500 shares for £20,000 in March 2015.

His chargeable gain is:

£

Test 4

Mildred bought 6,000 shares in George plc in June 2010 for £15,000. There was a 1 for 3 bonus issue in August 2011. Mildred sold 8,000 shares for £22,000 in December 2014.

Her chargeable gain is:

£

Test 5

What are the share matching rules for company shareholders?

Test 6

Q Ltd bought 10,000 shares in R plc in May 2003 at a cost of £90,000. There was a 1 for 4 rights issue in June 2009 at the cost of £12 per share and Q Ltd took up all of its rights entitlement.

Q Ltd sold 10,000 shares in R plc for £150,000 in January 2015.

The indexed rise between May 2003 and June 2009 is 0.176 and between June 2009 and January 2015 is 0.216.

(1) Using the proforma layout provided, show the share pool.

		No of shares	Cost	Indexed cost

(2) Using the proforma layout provided, compute the gain on sale.

	£

chapter 15:
RELIEFS FOR CHARGEABLE GAINS

chapter coverage 📖

In this chapter we consider three reliefs for chargeable gains. All three of the reliefs are available to individuals, however only rollover relief (replacement of business assets) is available to a company.

Entrepreneurs' relief reduces the rate of CGT on the disposal of certain business assets by an individual, to 10%.

The basic principle of the other two reliefs is that a gain is deferred by deducting it from a base cost to be used to calculate a future gain. This lower base cost causes a larger gain to arise in the future. The deferred gain is often said to be 'held-over' or 'rolled-over'.

The topics that we shall cover are:

✍ Entrepreneurs' relief

✍ Replacement of business assets or rollover relief

✍ Gift relief

ENTREPRENEURS' RELIEF

Introduction

Individuals can claim entrepreneurs' relief to reduce the rate of CGT on a material disposal of business assets. Gains on assets qualifying for entrepreneurs' relief are **taxed at 10%** regardless of the level of a person's taxable income.

Lifetime limit

There is a lifetime limit of £10 million of gains on which entrepreneurs' relief can be claimed.

HOW IT WORKS

Carrie has made several disposals qualifying for entrepreneurs' relief. The gains on these disposals are as follows:

1 May 2014	£7,750,000
1 June 2014	£2,300,000
1 February 2015	£2,200,000

Entrepreneurs' relief will be given on the following amounts:

1 May 2014 £7,750,000 (less than the lifetime limit of £10,000,000)

1 June 2014 £2,250,000 (lifetime limit £10,000,000 less relief already used of £7,750,000). £50,000 is not eligible for relief.

1 February 2015 None of the lifetime limit left therefore £2,200,000 is not eligible for entrepreneurs' relief.

Conditions for entrepreneurs' relief

Entrepreneurs' relief is available where there is a **material disposal of business assets**.

A material disposal of business assets is:

(a)   A **disposal of the whole or part of a business** that has been **owned by the individual** throughout the **period of one year** ending with the date of the disposal.

(b)   A **disposal of one or more assets** in use for the **purposes of a business** at the time at which the **business ceases** to be carried on provided that:

(i)   **The business was owned by the individual** throughout the **period of one year** ending with the date on which the business ceases to be carried on.

(ii)   **The assets are disposed of within three years** of the cessation of the business.

(c)   A **disposal of shares** or securities of a company where the company is the **individual's personal company**; the company is a **trading company**; the **individual is an officer** (eg a director) or employee of the company and these conditions are met either:

(i)   Throughout the period of one year ending with the date of the disposal.

(ii)   Throughout the period of one year ending with the date on which the company ceases to be a trading company and that date is within the period of three years ending with the date of the disposal.

For condition (a) to apply, there has to be a disposal of the whole or part of the business as a going concern, not just a disposal of individual assets. A business includes one carried on as a partnership of which the individual is a partner.

For both conditions (a) and (b):

■   The business must be a trade, profession or vocation conducted on a commercial basis with a view to the realisation of profits.

■   Relief is only available on relevant business assets. These are assets used for the purposes of the business and cannot include shares and securities or assets held as investments.

For condition (c), a personal company in relation to an individual is one where:

(a)   The individual holds at least 5% of the ordinary share capital.

(b)   The individual can exercise at least 5% of the voting rights in the company by virtue of that holding of shares.

Task 1

The following assets are disposed of in 2014/15 by various individuals. Identify which, if any, are qualifying disposals for entrepreneurs' relief. Tick the relevant box.

	✓
Part of a business in which the individual has been a partner since August 2012	
A freehold factory which the individual uses in his business and has owned for 10 years	
Unquoted shares held by the individual in a personal trading company in which he is employed and which he has owned for the previous two years	
Quoted shares held by the individual in a personal trading company in which he is employed and which he has owned for the previous two years	

Operation of the relief

Where there is a material disposal of business assets that results in both gains and losses, losses are set off against gains to give a single gain on the disposal of the business assets.

The rate of tax on this chargeable gain is 10%.

HOW IT WORKS

Sally sells her business in August 2014, realising the following gains and losses:

	£
Goodwill	120,000
Machine	122,000
Workshop	(42,000)

All the assets qualify for entrepreneurs' relief and she has no other chargeable disposals in the year.

The CGT payable on the disposal is:

	£
Net gains £(120,000 + 122,000 − 42,000)	200,000
Less annual exempt amount	(11,000)
Taxable gains	189,000
CGT @ 10%	18,900

In order to use losses and the annual exempt amount in the most beneficial manner, they should be first set against gains that do not qualify for entrepreneurs' relief in order to save tax at either 18% or 28%.

HOW IT WORKS

Robbie started in business as a manufacturer of widgets in July 2003. He acquired a freehold workshop for £86,000 in May 2005. He used the workshop in his business. In August 2009, Robbie invested £40,000 of his business profits in shares in an investment company. He bought a machine for use in his business in January 2014 at a cost of £35,000.

In November 2014, Robbie sold his business to a larger competitor. The sale proceeds were apportioned to capital assets as follows.

	£
Goodwill	50,000
Workshop	125,000
Shares	80,500
Machine	38,000

Robbie also had a loss brought forward of £1,000, but made no other disposals in 2014/15. He is a higher rate taxpayer.

Robbie's CGT liability on the disposal is calculated as follows:

	£	£
Proceeds of goodwill	50,000	
Less cost	(nil)	50,000
Proceeds of workshop	125,000	
Less cost	(86,000)	39,000
Proceeds of machine (N1)	38,000	
Less cost	(35,000)	3,000
Gains qualifying for entrepreneurs' relief		92,000
Proceeds of shares (N2)	80,500	
Less cost	(40,000)	40,500
		132,500
Chargeable gains		
Less loss b/fwd		(1,000)
Less annual exempt amount		(11,000)
Taxable gains		120,500
CGT payable		
£92,000 × 10% (gains eligible for entrepreneurs' relief)		9,200
£28,500 (120,500 – 92,000) × 28% (other gains) (N3)		7,980
		17,180

Notes

1   The gain on the machine is eligible for entrepreneurs' relief even though it has not been owned for one year. The condition is that the individual has owned the business for one year.

2   The gain on the shares is not eligible for entrepreneurs' relief because the shares are not relevant business assets.

3   The loss brought forward and the annual exempt amount are set against the gains not eligible for entrepreneurs' relief.

Unused basic rate band

In Chapter 12, of this Text, we established that if an individual is a basic rate taxpayer then CGT is payable at 18% on taxable gains up to the amount of the taxpayer's unused basic rate band and at 28% on the excess.

Although chargeable gains that qualify for entrepreneurs' relief are always taxed at a rate of 10%, they must be taken into account when establishing the rate to apply to other capital gains. Chargeable gains qualifying for entrepreneurs' relief therefore reduce the amount of any unused basic rate band.

HOW IT WORKS

(a)   Steve sells his business, all the assets of which qualify for entrepreneurs' relief, in August 2014. The gains arising are £15,000. He also sold investments in November 2014 realising chargeable gains of £40,000. £10,000 of Steve's basic rate band is unused for 2014/15.

The CGT payable is:

	£
Gains eligible for entrepreneurs' relief	15,000
Other gains	40,000
Chargeable gains	55,000
Less annual exempt amount (set against other gains)	(11,000)
Taxable gains	44,000

CGT payable	
£15,000 × 10% (gains eligible for entrepreneurs' relief)	1,500
£29,000 × 28% (other gains less annual exempt amount)	8,120
	9,620

The taxable gains eligible for entrepreneurs' relief exceeded Steve's unused basic rate band so the other gains, after the deduction of the annual exempt amount, are taxable at 28%.

(b) Sam sells his business, all the assets of which qualify for entrepreneurs' relief, in August 2014. The gains arising are £15,000. He also sold investments in November 2014 realising chargeable gains of £40,000. £20,000 of Sam's basic rate band was unused.

The CGT payable is:

	£
Gains eligible for entrepreneurs' relief	15,000
Other gains	40,000
Chargeable gains	55,000
Less annual exempt amount (set against other gains)	(11,000)
Taxable gains	44,000
CGT payable	
£15,000 × 10% (gains eligible for entrepreneurs' relief)	1,500
£5,000 × 18% (£20,000 − £15,000 of Sam's basic rate band is unused)	900
£24,000 × 28% (balance of other gains)	6,720
	9,120

Task 2

Gwynneth made the following gains on disposals during 2014/15:

19 July 2014 shares qualifying for entrepreneurs' relief   £50,000

25 November 2014 investments   £33,000

£4,000 of Gwynneth's basic rate band is unused.

The CGT payable by Gwynneth is:

£ [ ]

Claim

An individual must claim entrepreneurs' relief. **The claim deadline is the first anniversary of 31 January following the end of the tax year of disposal.** For a 2014/15 disposal, the taxpayer must claim by 31 January 2017.

Task 3

Lewis bought 10,000 ordinary shares in V Ltd in May 2004 for £50,000 which was a 10% holding. V Ltd is a trading company and Lewis was appointed as a director of the company in June 2006. He bought a further 1,000 shares for £10,000 in August 2011.

Lewis sold 2,200 of his shares in July 2014 for £33,500.

During 2014/15 he also realised a gain on the sale of a painting of £17,000, and had losses brought forward of £1,300. He has £3,400 of his basic rate band remaining unused.

(1) Using the proforma layout provided, show the share pool of shares in V Ltd owned by Lewis after the disposal in July 2014.

	No of shares	Cost £
May 2004 Acquisition		
August 2011 Acquisition		
July 2014 Disposal		
c/f		

(2) Using the proforma layout provided, calculate the CGT payable for 2014/15.

	£
Shares:	
Proceeds of sale	
Less allowable cost	
Gain (eligible for entrepreneurs' relief)	
Painting (not eligible for entrepreneurs' relief)	
Less loss b/fwd	
Less annual exempt amount	
Taxable gain	
CCT payable	
Shares:	
Painting:	

REPLACEMENT OF BUSINESS ASSETS/ROLLOVER RELIEF

ROLLOVER RELIEF is available to **both individuals and companies.**

A gain may be 'rolled-over' where it arises **on the disposal of a business asset** (the 'old' asset) **if another business asset** (the 'new' asset) **is acquired.**

The following conditions must be met:

- The old asset and the new asset must **both be used in a trade**.

- The old asset and the new asset must **both be qualifying assets**. Qualifying assets include:

   – Land and buildings used for the purpose of the trade
   – Fixed (that is, immoveable) plant and machinery
   – Goodwill (for individuals only)

- **Reinvestment** of the proceeds of the old asset must take place in a period beginning **one year before** and ending **three years after** the date of the disposal.

- For **all the gain** to be deferred **all the proceeds** of the old asset must be reinvested in the new asset.

- The 'new' asset can be one asset or more than one asset.

The new asset can be for use in a different trade from the old asset. **Deferral is usually obtained by deducting the gain on the old asset from the cost of the new asset.**

HOW IT WORKS

A freehold factory was purchased by a sole trader on 13 May 2001 for £60,000 and sold for £90,000 on 18 September 2014. A replacement factory was purchased on 6 December 2014 for £100,000. Rollover relief was claimed on the sale of the first factory.

(a) *Gain on sale September 2014*

	£
Disposal proceeds	90,000
Less cost	(60,000)
Gain (to defer all proceeds re-invested)	30,000

(b) *Revised base cost of asset purchased in December 2014*

Original cost	100,000
Less rolled over gain	(30,000)
Revised base cost (this will be used to calculate gain on subsequent sale of new asset)	70,000

Task 4

George bought a freehold factory for business use in August 2009 for £35,000. It was sold in March 2015 for £90,000. A replacement factory was purchased in April 2014 for £120,000 and rollover relief was claimed.

(1) The gain on the sale of the factory in March 2015 is:

£ [   ]

(2) The gain that can be rolled over is:

£ [   ]

(3) The base cost of the new factory acquired in April 2014 is:

£ [   ]

Task 5

Louis bought office premises for £80,000 in July 2010. He sold them for £100,000 in May 2014. Louis bought a freehold factory for use in his business in June 2014 at a cost of £350,000 and claimed rollover relief in respect of the gain on the office premises. Louis sold the factory for £375,000 in September 2016.

(1) The gain on the sale of the office premises in May 2014 is:

£ [   ]

(2) The gain rolled over into the factory is:

£ [   ]

(3) The gain on the sale of the factory in September 2016 is:

£ [   ]

Sale proceeds not fully reinvested

If the proceeds of the sale of an asset are not fully reinvested in a new qualifying asset, **an amount of the gain equal to the proceeds not reinvested is immediately chargeable.** The balance of the gain can be rolled over.

If the amount of proceeds not reinvested exceeds the gain, no amount of the gain can therefore be rolled over. This is the same as saying the amount chargeable is the lower of the gain and the amount not reinvested.

HOW IT WORKS

Susannah realised a gain of £300,000 on the disposal of an office block used in her business. The office block was sold for £700,000. A new office block factory was bought for £600,000 in the following month.

The proceeds not reinvested are £100,000 so this amount of the gain is immediately chargeable. The remaining gain of £200,000 can be rolled over and set against the base cost of the new office block. This means the base cost of the new office block is £(600,000 – 200,000) = £400,000.

Task 6

A sole trader sold a factory in July 2014 for £670,000 realising a gain of £120,000. In September 2014 a replacement factory was bought for £650,000.

Advise the sole trader as to whether a chargeable gain will arise on the sale of the first factory. Assume rollover relief is claimed where possible and explain the implications of this for the future sale of the replacement factory.

HOW IT WORKS

D Ltd acquired a factory in April 2009 at a cost of £120,000. It used the factory in its trade throughout the period of its ownership.

In August 2014, D Ltd sold the factory for £210,000. In November 2014, it acquired another factory at a cost of £180,000.

The indexed rise between April 2009 and August 2014 is 0.219.

The gain on sale is:

	£
Proceeds	210,000
Less cost	(120,000)
	90,000
Less indexation allowance 0.219 × £120,000	(26,280)
	63,720
Less rollover relief (balancing figure)	(33,720)
Chargeable gain: amount not reinvested £(210,000 – 180,000)	30,000

The base cost of the new factory is:

	£
Cost of second factory	180,000
Less rolled over gain	(33,720)
Base cost	146,280

Task 7

H Ltd acquired a warehouse in May 2008 for £75,000. It used the warehouse in its trade throughout the period of its ownership.

H Ltd sold the warehouse for £120,000 in August 2014. It had acquired a workshop for £100,000 in March 2014.

The indexed rise between May 2008 and August 2014 is 0.199.

(1) The gain on sale of the warehouse in August 2014 assuming that rollover relief is claimed is:

£ [ ]

(2) The base cost of the workshop is:

£ [ ]

GIFT RELIEF

Individuals can claim GIFT RELIEF to defer a gain otherwise arising **on the gift of a business asset.**

The gift is deemed to be made at market value.

The transferee is deemed to acquire the asset for its market value less the deferred gain.

HOW IT WORKS

John bought a business asset in 2009 for £20,000. On 1 May 2014 John gave the asset to Marie Louise. The market value of the asset on the date of the gift was £90,000.

John is deemed to dispose of the asset for its market value of £90,000 so the gain arising on the gift is:

	£
Deemed disposal proceeds	90,000
Less cost	(20,000)
Gain	70,000

The gain of £70,000 is deferred by setting it against the value of £90,000 at which Marie Louise is deemed to acquire the gift. Therefore Marie Louise is deemed to acquire the gift for £20,000 (£90,000 - £70,000) and this will be used as the base cost for future disposals.

Task 8

Archie purchased business premises in July 2006 for £80,000. In December 2010 Archie gave the premises, then valued at £400,000, to Hugo and claimed gift relief. Hugo continued to run a business from the premises but decided to sell them in May 2014 for £675,000.

(1) The gift relief on the gift made in December 2010 is:

£	

(2) The gain on the sale in May 2014 is:

£	

Qualifying assets for gift relief purposes include:

(a) Assets used in a trade carried on:

(i) By the donor
(ii) By the donor's personal company

(b) Shares in:

(i) An unquoted trading company
(ii) The donor's personal trading company

A 'personal company' is one in which not less than 5% of the voting rights are controlled by the donor.

Task 9

Deidre gives the following assets to Steve.

Which, if any, are qualifying assets for the purposes of gift relief?

	✓
An antique painting	
Quoted shares in a trading company of which Deidre controls 1%	
Unquoted trading company shares	
A freehold factory that Deidre has always used in her printing business	

Task 10

Julie bought 10,000 shares in an unquoted trading company for £50,000 in July 2006. Julie gave her shares to Jack in May 2014 when they were worth £85,000. Jack sold the shares for £95,000 in December 2014.

(1) If gift relief is not claimed, Julie's chargeable gain is:

£ [　　　　　　　]

and Jack's chargeable gain is:

£ [　　　　　　　]

(2) If gift relief is claimed, Julie's chargeable gain is:

£ [　　　　　　　]

and Jack's chargeable gain is:

£ [　　　　　　　]

Assessment focus

In the live assessment you will be provided with 'Taxation Data' that can be accessed through pop up windows. The content of these taxation data tables has been reproduced at the front of this Text.

The rate and limit for entrepreneurs' relief covered in this chapter are included within 'taxation data 1'. Make sure you familiarise yourself with the content and practise referring to it as you work through this Text.

The information included in this chapter typically will be tested in the following task:

Task 11 – Capital gains tax exemptions, losses, relief and tax payable

Performance feedback

The feedback given below relates to students' performance on the AQ2010 version of the assessments. However, the points made by the assessor will be equally as valid for students who will be sitting the assessment under AQ2013.

Task 2.4 (AQ2010)

Capital gains tax reliefs including losses, annual exempt amount and entrepreneurs' relief are all within this task. Only 40% of students achieved competence illustrating a lack of robust preparation for the topics covered. Entrepreneurs' relief causes the most issues, yet the extent of this topic covered in the standards is really quite basic.

In many instances, students are simply not reading the question right. For example, if a question asks how much of a gain would be taxable at 10% if applicable for entrepreneurs' relief, too many students will try to compute the actual tax payable. The question does not ask for this, and what the student is doing is more complex than is actually needed.

Task 2.5 (AQ2010)

Fortunately, this is a small task carrying relatively few marks. This comment is made as it is by far the worst answered task in the whole assessment, with only 20% of students being deemed competent. The only topic covered in these tasks is rollover relief and it is simply not covered adequately.

The topic itself is quite straightforward, but it would appear that students try to jump at the answer rather than working it out logically.

CHAPTER OVERVIEW

- Entrepreneurs' relief reduces the rate of CGT on gains made by an individual on certain business disposals to 10%

- There is a lifetime limit of £10 million for entrepreneurs' relief

- Entrepreneurs' relief applies to disposals of an unincorporated business (or part of a business), disposals of business assets on cessation, and shares in a trading company that is the individual's personal company and of which he is an officer or employee

- Rollover relief can be used by individuals and companies to defer a gain when a qualifying business asset is replaced with another qualifying business asset

- Qualifying business assets for rollover relief include land and buildings, fixed plant and machinery and, for individuals, goodwill. Both the old and the new assets must be used for the purposes of a trade

- If sale proceeds are not fully reinvested, an amount of the gain equal to the proceeds not reinvested is immediately chargeable. The remainder of the gain may be rolled over

- The rolled over gain reduces the cost of the new asset

- The new asset must be acquired in the period commencing one year before and ending three years after the disposal

- Gift relief can be used by an individual to defer a gain on the gift of business assets

- The transferee acquires the gift at its market value less the amount of the deferred gain

- Qualifying assets for gift relief include assets used in a trade by the donor or his personal company, unquoted shares in a trading company and shares in a personal trading company

Keywords

Entrepreneurs' relief – Reduces the effective rate of tax on the disposal of certain business assets from 18% or 28% to 10%

Rollover relief – Can defer a gain when business assets are replaced

Gift relief – Can defer a gain on a gift of business assets by an individual

TEST YOUR LEARNING

Test 1

Ian sold his business as a going concern to John in May 2014. The gains on sale were £10,400,000. Ian had not previously made any claims for entrepreneurs' relief, and made no other disposals in 2014/15. Ian is a higher rate taxpayer.

Ian's CGT liability for 2014/15 is:

£	

Test 2

Jemma sold her shareholding in J Ltd in January 2015. She had acquired the shares in August 2005 for £10,000. The proceeds of sale were £80,000. The disposal qualified for entrepreneurs' relief.

Jemma's CGT on the disposal, assuming she has already used the annual exempt amount for 2014/15, is:

£	

Test 3

K Ltd sold a factory on 10 November 2014. It purchased the following assets:

Date of purchase	Asset
21 September 2013	Office block
15 February 2015	Freehold factory
4 June 2016	Fork lift truck
8 December 2017	Freehold warehouse

All of the above assets are used for the purpose of the trade of K Ltd.

Against which purchase may K Ltd claim rollover relief in respect of the gain arising on disposal of the factory?

	✓
Office block	
Freehold factory	
Fork lift truck	
Freehold warehouse	

Test 4

Trevor bought land for £100,000 in March 2006. In March 2014, this land was sold for £400,000 and replacement land was bought for £380,000. The replacement land was sold in May 2015 for £500,000. Both pieces of land were used in Trevor's trade, which is still continuing.

What is the chargeable gain arising in May 2015? Assume all available reliefs were claimed.

	✓
£120,000	
£200,000	
£400,000	
£420,000	

Test 5

Decide whether the following statement is True or False.

Provided both assets are used in Mr Astro's trade, a gain arising on the sale of freehold land and buildings can be rolled over against the cost of goodwill.

	✓
True	
False	

Test 6

A company sells freehold land and buildings in 2014.

If relief for replacement of business assets is to be claimed, reinvestment of the proceeds must take place in a period beginning

months before and ending

months after the date of disposal

Test 7

H Ltd sells a warehouse for £400,000. The warehouse cost £220,000 and the indexation allowance available is £40,000. The company acquires another warehouse ten months later for £375,000 and claims rollover relief.

The chargeable gain after rollover relief is:

£	

Test 8

Decide whether the following statement is True or False.

If Sara gives some jewellery to her daughter Emily, gift relief can be claimed.

	✓
True	
False	

Test 9

Tommy gave Sinbad a factory in June 2014 that had been used in his trade. The factory cost £50,000 in October 2005 and was worth £200,000 at the date of the gift. Sinbad sold the factory for £350,000 in May 2015.

If gift relief is claimed, the gain on the gift by Tommy is:

£

and the gain on the sale by Sinbad is:

£

CHAPTER 1   The tax framework

1

£	20,750

	Non-savings income £	Savings income £	Dividend income £	Total £
Trading income	16,000			
Building society interest		6,000		
Dividends			8,750	
Net income	16,000	6,000	8,750	30,750
Less personal allowance	(10,000)			(10,000)
Taxable income	6,000	6,000	8,750	**20,750**

2

£	13,627

	£
£31,865 × 20%	6,373
£18,135 × 40%	7,254
£50,000	**13,627**

3

£	8,843

	£
Non-savings income	
£1,500 × 20%	300
Savings income	
£1,380 × 10%	138
£28,620 × 20%	5,724
£30,000	
Dividend income	
£365 × 10%	37
£8,135 × 32.5%	2,644
£8,500	**8,843**

4

£	60,752

	£
Non-savings income	
£31,865 × 20%	6,373
£88,135 × 40%	35,254
£120,000	
Dividend income	
£30,000 × 32.5%	9,750
£25,000 × 37.5%	9,375
£55,000	**60,752**

CHAPTER 2   Computing trading income

1

	£
Profit for the year in accounts	38,000
Add entertaining expenses	2,000
Add depreciation	4,000
	44,000
Less capital allowances	(3,500)
Taxable trading profit	**40,500**

2

	Revenue	Capital
Paying employee wages	✓	
Paying rent for premises	✓	
Buying machinery		✓
Buying a van		✓
Building an extension to shop		✓
Paying for repairs to car	✓	

3

	✓
True	
False	✓

As the cinema was usable on acquisition the repair expenditure is allowable. This point was decided in the case of *Odeon Associated Theatres v Jones*. You do not need to remember case names for assessment purposes.

4

£	240

£240 (40% × £600) must be added back in computing taxable trading profits.

5

Amount to add back	✓
£100	✓
£280	
£380	
None	

HMRC allow the deduction of donations to small local charities.

6

Amount to add back	✓
£7,000	✓
£9,000	
£10,500	
£8,500	

The expenses relating to the employee service contracts are allowable as this is a revenue item.

The expenses relating to the purchase of new offices are disallowable as they relate to a capital item. Legal expenses relating to the renewal of a short lease are specifically allowable.

7

Amount to add back	✓
£17,450	
£16,000	
£18,450	✓
£11,450	

The redundancy payments are allowable. The payment of a salary to the proprietor of a business is not deductible because it is just a method of extracting a profit from the business and that profit is taxable in the normal way as part of the taxable trading profits. 15% of leasing costs of car with CO_2 emissions exceeding 130g/km are disallowable.

8

£	560

	£
Heating (70% × £800)	**560**

The private portion of the above bill must be added back in computing taxable trading profits.

9

Expenditure	£	Add back ✓
Staff tennis outing for 30 employees	1,800	
2,000 tee shirts with firm's logo given to race runners	4,500	
Advertising and sponsorship of an athletic event	2,000	
Entertaining customers	7,300	✓
Staff Christmas party (30 employees)	2,400	

10

	£	£
Profit for the year in accounts		22,710
Add: Depreciation charge	1,500	
Provision against a fall in raw material prices	5,000	
Entertainment expenses	750	
Legal expenses (relate to a capital item)	250	
		7,500
		30,210
Less rental income received (to tax as property income)		(860)
Adjusted trading profit		29,350

CHAPTER 3 Capital allowances

1

	Allowable (revenue based) ✓	Disallowable (capital related) ✓
Rent paid on premises	✓	
Purchase of an office		✓
Purchase of machinery		✓
Repairs to machinery	✓	
Redecoration of premises	✓	
Depreciation charge on machinery		✓

2 (1) The AIA can be claimed on:

	Claim	Not claim
Computer system	✓	☐
Machinery for factory	✓	☐
Factory extension	☐	✓
Motor car for director	☐	✓

(2) The eligible expenditure of £177,000 does not exceed the maximum amount of the AIA of £500,000 for the year. The maximum claim that can be made is

£	177,000

3

The maximum AIA available for the year to 31 December 2014 is

£	437,500

£250,000 × 3/12 = £62,500 (for the period up to 5 April 2014) + £500,000 × 9/12 = £375,000 (for the period from 6 April 2014) = £437,500

The maximum AIA that Mr Blonde can claim for the year to 31 December 2014 is

£	355,000

The amount of expenditure incurred is less than the maximum AIA available.

4

The maximum AIA available for the year to 30 June 2014 is:

> £ | 312,500

£250,000 × 9/12 = £187,500 (for the period up to 31 March 2014) + £500,000 × 3/12 = £125,000 (for the period from 1 April 2015) = £312,500

The maximum AIA that Orange Ltd can claim for the year to 30 June 2014 is

> £ | 312,500

The amount of expenditure incurred of £450,000 exceeds the maximum AIA available for the year. Only £312,500 of AIA can be claimed but the remaining £137,500 of expenditure will be eligible for writing down allowances.

5

	Main pool £	Allowances £
Year end 5 April 2015		
B/f	10,000	
Addition (no AIA on car)	8,000	
Disposal	(6,000)	
	12,000	
WDA @ 18%	(2,160)	2,160
C/f	9,840	

6

	AIA £	Main pool £	Allowances £
Year end 5 April 2015			
B/f		12,000	
AIA additions			
Machinery	488,000		
Furniture	21,000		
	509,000		
AIA	(500,000)		500,000
	9,000		
Transfer to main pool	(9,000)	9,000	
		21,000	
WDA@ 18%		(3,780)	3,780
C/f		17,220	
Capital allowances			503,780

7

Year end 5 April 2015	Main pool £	Allowance £
B/f	47,000	
Less disposal (restricted to cost)	(7,000)	
	40,000	
WDA @ 18%	(7,200)	7,200
C/f	32,800	

8

3 m/e 31 March 2015	Main pool £	Allowance £
B/f	20,000	
Non AIA addition	4,000	
	24,000	
WDA @ 18% × 3/12	(1,080)	1,080
C/f	22,920	

9

8 m/e 31 December 2014	AIA £	Main pool £	Allowances £
B/f		12,000	
AIA additions			
14.6.14 Furniture	135,000		
15.8.14 Machinery	255,000		
	390,000		
AIA £500,000 × 8/12	(333,333)		333,333
	56,667		
Transfer to main pool	(56,667)	56,667	
		68,667	
WDA@ 18% × 8/12		(8,240)	8,240
C/f		60,427	
Capital allowances			341,573

The AIA and WDA are prorated in the short period.

10

10 months ended 5 April 2015	Special rate pool £	Allowances £
Addition	18,000	
WDA £18,000 @ 8% × 10/12	(1,200)	1,200
C/f	16,800	

11

	Private use asset		Allowances 75%
	£		£
Year ended 5 April 2015			
Car	20,000		
WDA £20,000 @ 8%	(1,600)	× 75%	1,200
C/f	18,400		

CHAPTER 4 Taxing unincorporated businesses

1

	✓
1 October 2014 to 30 September 2015	
1 April 2014 to 31 March 2015	
1 October 2013 to 30 September 2014	✓
6 April 2014 to 5 April 2015	

2

Tax year	Basis period	Taxable profits £
2013/14	1 June 2013 to 5 April 2014	10,000
2014/15	1 June 2013 to 31 May 2014	12,000
2015/16	1 June 2014 to 31 May 2015	21,000

In 2013/14 the taxable profits are £12,000 × 10/12 = £10,000

3　(1)

Tax year	Basis period	Taxable profits £
2012/13	1 March 2013 to 5 April 2013	2,000
2013/14	6 April 2013 to 5 April 2014	24,000
2014/15	1 July 2013 to 30 June 2014	24,000
2015/16	1 July 2014 to 30 June 2015	36,800

In 2012/13, taxable profits are £32,000 × 1/16 = £2,000
In 2013/14, taxable profits are £32,000 × 12/16 =£24,000
In 2014/15, taxable profits are £32,000 × 12/16 =£24,000

(2)　The overlap profits are:

£	18,000

1 July 2013 to 5 April 2014 (£32,000 × 9/16)

4

Tax year	Basis period	Taxable profits £
2012/13	y/e 30.6.12	12,000
2013/14	y/e 30.6.13	8,000
2014/15	1.7.13 to 31.1.15	11,000

In 2014/15 taxable profits are £6,000 + £5,000 = £11,000

5

Tax year	Basis period	Taxable profits £
2010/11	1 May 2010 to 5 April 2011	13,750
2011/12	1 May 2010 to 30 April 2011	15,000
2012/13	1 May 2011 to 30 April 2012	9,000
2013/14	1 May 2012 to 30 April 2013	10,500
2014/15	1 May 2013 to 31 January 2015	3,200
Total taxable trading profits		51,450

In 2010/11 taxable profits are (£15,000 × 11/12) = £13,750

Overlap profits 1 May 2010 to 5 April 2011 (£15,000 × 11/12) = £13,750. This amount is deducted in the final year of trading.

In 2014/15 taxable profits are (£16,000 + £950 − £13,750) = £3,200

CHAPTER 5 Partnerships

1 The taxable trading profit for Roger for the year to 31 December 2014 is:

£	150,000

and the taxable trading profit for Muggles for the year to 31 December 2014 is:

£	60,000

Working:	Total £	Roger £	Muggles £
Salaries	60,000	30,000	30,000
Profit (210,000 – 60,000) 4:1	150,000	120,000	30,000
Taxable trading profits	210,000	**150,000**	**60,000**

2

	Total £	James £	Kieran £	Jemima £
Interest on capital (20,000 × 5%)	3,000	1,000	1,000	1,000
Salaries	70,000	0	35,000	35,000
Division of profits 3:1:1	197,000	118,200	39,400	39,400
Taxable trading profits	270,000	119,200	75,400	75,400

3

	£
1 July 2013 to 31 March 2014 (80,000 x 9/12)	60,000
1 April 2014 to 30 June 2014 (80,000 x 3/12)	20,000
Total profits	80,000

	Total £	Hansel £	Greta £
1 July 2013 to 31 March 2014 (1:1)	60,000	30,000	30,000
1 April 2014 to 30 June 2014 (4:1)	20,000	16,000	4,000
	80,000	46,000	34,000

4

	Total	New partner (30%)
	£	£
Year ended 31 October 2013		
1 November 2012 to 31 May 2013 (7/12)	19,950	–
1 June 2013 to 31 October 2013 (5/12)	14,250	4,275
	34,200	
Year ended 31 October 2014	45,600	13,680

His taxable profits for 2013/14 are:

£	£9,975

(1 June 2013 to 5 April 2014) £4,275 + 5/12 × £13,680

His overlap profits carried forward are:

£	£5,700

(5/12 × £13,680)

His taxable profits for 2014/15 are:

£	£13,680

(year ended 31 October 2014)

5

	Total £	X £	Y £	Z £
Year ended 31 March 2013	24,000	8,000	8,000	8,000
Year ended 31 March 2014				
1 April 2013 to 30 June 2013 (3/12)	3,500	1,167	1,167	1,166
1 July 2013 to 31 March 2014 (9/12)	10,500	0	6,300	4,200
	14,000	1,167	7,467	5,366
Year ended 31 March 2015	48,000	0	28,800	19,200

Y and Z are taxed on a continuing basis of assessment throughout.

2013/14 is the final tax year for X whose assessment is for the period 1 April 2013 to 30 June 2013. X has no overlap profits to deduct.

	X	Y	Z
2012/13 (y/e 31 March 2013)	8,000	8,000	8,000
2013/14 (y/e 31 March 2014)	1,167	7,467	5,366
2014/15 (y/e 31 March 2015)	0	28,800	19,200

CHAPTER 6   Computing taxable total profits

1   (1)   Capital allowances

	Main pool £	Allowances £
B/f	21,500	
Addition (no AIA on cars)	11,000	
	32,500	
WDA @ 18%	(5,850)	5,850
C/f	26,650	

No adjustment for private use in a company's capital allowances computation.

(2)   Trading profits

	£
Profit for the year	429,000
Less property business income	(4,000)
Less capital allowances (W2)	(5,850)
Trading profits	419,150

(3)   Taxable total profits

	£
Trading profits	419,150
Property business income	4,000
Taxable total profits	423,150

2

£	80,250

	£
Trading profits	85,000
Interest income £(6,000 + 1,500)	7,500
Chargeable gains	2,950
Less qualifying charitable donation	(15,200)
Taxable total profits	**80,250**

Note. Dividends received do not form part of taxable total profits.

3

	Year ended 31 March 2015	3 months ended 30 June 2015
	£	£
Trading profits (12/15 : 3/15)	240,000	60,000
Interest accrued	6,000	1,500
Chargeable gain	250,000	0
Qualifying charitable donation	(50,000)	0
Taxable total profits	446,000	61,500

CHAPTER 7 Computing corporation tax payable

1

£	65,000

	£
Taxable total profits	60,000
Dividends (× 100/90)	5,000
Augmented profits	**65,000**

2

£	441,000

	£
Taxable total profits	2,100,000
Dividend (45,000 × 100/90)	50,000
Augmented profits	2,150,000

The main rate of CT applies: £2,100,000 × 21%

Note that although augmented profits are used to work out the rate of tax that applies, CT is only charged on taxable total profits.

3 (1)

	£
Taxable total profits	220,000
Dividends (× 100/90)	100,000
Augmented profits	320,000

(2) Marginal relief applies.

	£
£220,000 × 21%	46,200
Less 1/400 £(1,500,000 - 320,000) × $\dfrac{220,000}{320,000}$	(2,028)
CT liability	44,172

4

£	12,000

Taxable total profits/augmented profits

£
60,000

The small profits rate applies.

CT liability £60,000 × 20% = £12,000

5

£	266,600

(1) Augmented profits are £1,590,000

This means main rate of CT applies

(2) With a year ended 31 December 2014, 3 months fall into FY13 and 9 months fall into FY14.

(3) Tax on taxable total profits (FY 2013)

£1,240,000 x 3/12 × 23% =£71,300

Tax on taxable total profits (FY 2014)

£1,240,000 x 9/12 × 21% =£195,300

Total CT liability = £71,300 + £195,300 = **£266,600**

6

(1) A Ltd's augmented profits for the period ended 31 December 2014 are:

£	250,000

£200,000 + (45,000 × 100/90)

(2) The lower limit applicable is:

£	225,000

£300,000 × 9/12

and the upper limit applicable is:

£	1,125,000

£1,500,000 × 9/12

(3) A Ltd's corporation tax liability for the nine month period to 31 December 2014 is:

£	40,250

(3) Marginal relief applies:

	£
All of the 9 months fall into FY14	
£200,000 × 21%	42,000
Less	
1/400 £(**1,125,000** – 250,000) × £200/£250	(1,750)
Corporation tax liability	**40,250**

Note that the reduced upper limit is used in the marginal relief calculation.

7

(1) S Ltd's augmented profits for the year ended 31 March 2015 are:

£	385,000

(2) The lower limit applicable is:

£	100,000

£300,000/3

and the upper limit applicable is:

£	500,000

£1,500,000/3

(3) S Ltd's corporation tax liability for the year to 31 March 2015 is:

£	75,331

Marginal relief applies:

	£
FY14	
£360,000 × 21%	75,600
Less 1/400 £(500,000 – 385,000) × $\dfrac{360,000}{385,000}$	(269)
CT liability	**75,331**

CHAPTER 8   Losses

1

		£
Total income		21,000
Less loss		(21,000)
Net income		NIL

Loss c/f £30,000 – £21,000 =

£	(9,000)

The loss is deducted from total income to compute net income. Since the personal allowance is deducted from net income, the benefit of the personal allowance is wasted.

2

(1)   The taxable total profits for the year to 31 March 2015 are:

£	27,000

	£
Trading profits	40,000
Less carry forward loss relief	(40,000)
	NIL
Property business income	25,000
Chargeable gain	2,000
Taxable total profits	**27,000**

Losses carried forward can be set only against the trading profits. They cannot be set against other profits.

(2)   What amount, if any, of the trading losses remain to be carried forward at 1 April 2015?

£	(10,000)

(£50,000 – £40,000) remain to be carried forward at 1 April 2015.

3

	Year ended 31 March 2014 £	Year ended 31 March 2015 £	Year ended 31 March 2016 £
Trading profits	70,000	0	60,000
Less c/fwd loss relief	0	0	(60,000)(iii)
Property income	10,000	10,000	10,000
Total profits	80,000	10,000	10,000
Less CY and C/B loss relief	(80,000)(ii)	(10,000)(i)	0
Less qualifying charitable donation	0	0	(10,000)
Taxable total profits	0	0	0
Unrelieved qualifying charitable donation	10,000	30,000	5,000

(3) The trading loss to carry forward is:

£ | 10,000

(£160,000 − £10,000 − £80,000 − £60,000)

4

| | Year ended 31 October | | |
	2012 £	2013 £	2014 £
Trading profits	50,000	40,000	0
Bank interest	10,000	5,000	5,000
Chargeable gain £(12,000 – 7,000)	0	0	5,000
Total profits	60,000	45,000	10,000
Less current period loss relief	0	0	(10,000)
carry back loss relief	0	(45,000)	0
Taxable total profits	60,000	0	0

The capital loss has to be carried forward to set against the future chargeable gain. It cannot be set against other profits.

The trading loss to carry forward is:

£	(35,000)

(90,000 – 10,000 – 45,000)

CHAPTER 9   National Insurance

1

Class 2

£	143	.	00

(52 × £2.75)

Class 4

£	1,533	.	96

9% × (£25,000 − 7,956)

2

Class 2

£	143	.	00

(52 × £2.75)

Class 4

£	3,414	.	51

Working: £

9% × (£41,865 − £7,956)   3,051.81
2% × (£60,000 − 41,865)   362.70
                                                             3,414.51

CHAPTER 10 Self assessment for individuals

1

> 2 February 2016

Since the notice to file was issued after 31 October 2015, the filing date is three months after the notice was issued

2 Kelly's penalty can be reduced from 70% of the potential lost revenue (for a deliberate, but not concealed error) to 20%, with the unprompted disclosure of her error.

3 Each payment on account for 2015/16 will be

> £ | 7,000

(14,000 / 2)

They will be due on 31 January 2016 and 31 July 2016 .

CHAPTER 11   Self assessment for companies

1

30 September 2015

The later of:

(a)   30 September 2015
(b)   1 September 2015

2   The two accounting periods are:

Year ended 31 December 2013

and

Six months to 30 June 2014

Tax returns are required for both of these accounting periods. The due date for filing **both** returns is:

30 June 2015

3   The maximum penalty for late filing is:

£	1,000

The return is more than three but less than six months late so the penalty is £100 plus £10 a day for 90 days. If it had been more than six months late a tax geared penalty would also have been imposed.

4   The date by which HMRC may commence an enquiry into the return based on these accounts is:

31 March 2017

(The return was submitted before the filing due date)

5   The latest date by which HMRC can commence an enquiry into the company's return is:

31 January 2016

31 January, 30 April, 31 July or 31 October next following the anniversary of the actual filing date where the return is filed late.

6

	✓
14 October 2014	
14 July 2015	✓
31 July 2015	
1 January 2016	

As S Ltd is a large company instalments are due as follows:

14 October 2014

14 January 2015

14 April 2015

14 July 2015

CHAPTER 12 Chargeable gains – the basics

1

	Chargeable ✓	Exempt ✓
A diamond necklace	✓	
A cash sum invested in premium bonds that results in a substantial win		✓
A vintage Rolls Royce		✓

2 Jack's gain on sale is:

£	24,450

	£
Proceeds of sale	60,000
Less costs of disposal £(1,200 + 750)	(1,950)
Net proceeds of sale	58,050
Less original cost	(25,000)
costs of acquisition	(600)
enhancement expenditure	(8,000)
Chargeable gain	24,450

3 Tina's taxable gains for 2014/15 are:

£	7,000

(18,000 – £11,000)

4 The capital losses carried forward to 2015/16 are:

	✓
nil	
£4,000	
£3,000	
£2,000	✓

	£
Chargeable gains	13,000
Less allowable losses	(1,000)
	12,000
Less capital losses b/f (loss relief)	(1,000)
Net gain	11,000

Losses c/f £2,000 £(3,000 – 1,000)

5   The CGT payable for 2014/15 by Sarah is:

£	6,440

	£
Chargeable gains (£21,000 + £17,500)	38,500
Less loss	(4,500)
	34,000
Less annual exempt amount	(11,000)
Taxable gains	23,000
CGT payable	
£23,000 × 28%	6,440

6

	£
Proceeds	200,000
Cost	(80,000)
Indexation allowance (80,000 x 0.422)	(33,760)
Gain	86,240

7   The allowable loss is:

£	(30,000)

	£
Proceeds of sale	20,000
Less cost	(50,000)
Allowable loss	**(30,000)**

The indexation allowance cannot increase an allowable loss.

8   The gain/ loss is:

£	Nil

	£
Proceeds of sale	70,000
Less cost	(50,000)
Less indexation allowance 50,000 × 0.637 = 31,850, restricted to £20,000	(20,000)
Gain	0

The indexation allowance cannot create a loss.

CHAPTER 13 Further aspects of chargeable gains

1 The chargeable gain arising on the disposal is:

£	351,000

	£
Proceeds	400,000
Less costs of disposal	(9,000)
Net proceeds of sale	391,000
Less cost	
(400,000/400,000 + 600,000) × £100,000	(40,000)
Chargeable gain	351,000

2

	✓
True	
False	✓

No chargeable gain/allowable loss arises as greyhounds are exempt assets as they are wasting chattels.

3 The gain arising is:

	✓
nil	
£5,833	
£7,000	
£6,667	✓

	£
Gross proceeds	10,000
Less commission (5% x £10,000)	(500)
	9,500
Less cost	(2,500)
	7,000

Maximum gain 5/3 × £(10,000 – 6,000) = £6,667

4   The allowable loss is:

£	(3,200)

	£
	£
Deemed proceeds	6,000
Less commission (£3,600 × 10/90)	(400)
	5,600
Less cost	(8,800)
Allowable loss	(3,200)

5   (a)

The vase	£
Proceeds	7,000
Less selling expenses (£7,000 × 5%)	(350)
	6,650
Less cost	(800)
Chargeable gain	5,850

The gain is the lower of £5,850 and £(7,000 − 6,000) × 5/3 = £1,667, so it is __£1,667__.

(b)

The sideboard	£
Proceeds (deemed)	6,000
Less selling expenses (5,000 × 5%)	(250)
	5,750
Less cost	(7,000)
Allowable loss	(1,250)

6

(1)   The cost of the painting sold is:

£	33,803

(100,000/100,000+ 255,000) × £120,000 = **£33,803**

(2)   The chargeable gain arising on the disposal is:

£	46,366

	£
Gross proceeds	100,000
Less legal fees	(8,000)
Proceeds of sale (net)	92,000
Less cost (above)	(33,803)
	58,197
Less indexation allowance £33,803 × 0.350	(11,831)
Chargeable gain	46,366

7   The allowable loss arising on disposal of the painting by Holly is:

£	(10,000)

	£
Deemed proceeds (market value)	50,000
Less cost	(60,000)
Allowable loss	(10,000)

The loss may only be set against gains arising on the disposal of other assets by Holly to Emily in 2014/15 or future tax years.

8

	✓
nil	✓
£18,000	
£31,000	
£13,000	

William transfers the asset to his wife Kate on a 'no gain/no loss' basis. This assumes that William sold it for 'deemed proceeds' equal to his original cost ie £14,000. The market value and the actual proceeds received are not relevant.

CHAPTER 14   Share disposals

1   Noah will match his disposal of 15,000 shares on 17 June 2014 as follows:

1. 1,000 shares bought on 17 June 2014 (same day)

2. 2,000 shares bought on 19 June 2014 (next 30 days, FIFO basis)

3. 12,000 shares from the 20,000 shares in the share pool

2   The gain on the sale in 2015 is:

£ | 10,833

Share pool

	No of shares	Cost
		£
May 1999 Acquisition	9,000	4,500
August 2008 Disposal	(2,000)	(1,000)
(£4,500 × 2,000/9,000 = £1,000)		
c/f	7,000	3,500
May 2011 Acquisition	5,000	7,500
	12,000	11,000
January 2015 Disposal	(10,000)	(9,167)
(£11,000 × 10,000/12,000 = £9,167)		
c/f	2,000	1,833

Gain:

	£
Proceeds of sale	20,000
Less cost	(9,167)
Chargeable gain	**10,833**

3   Eliot will match the disposal of 6,000 shares on 25 July 2014 as follows:

    1. 1,000 shares bought on 25 July 2014 (same day)

    2. 500 shares bought on 27 July 2014 (next 30 days, FIFO basis)

    3. 4,500 shares from the 7,000 shares in the share pool

Disposal of 1,000 shares bought on 25 July 2014

	£
Proceeds of sale $\dfrac{1,000}{6,000} \times £21,600$	3,600
Less cost	(3,800)
Allowable loss	(200)

Disposal of 500 shares bought on 27 July 2014

	£
Proceeds of sale $\dfrac{500}{6,000} \times £21,600$	1,800
Less allowable cost	(1,700)
Chargeable gain	100

Disposal of 4,500 shares from the share pool

	£
Proceeds of sale $\dfrac{4,500}{6,000} \times £21,600$	16,200
Less allowable cost (W)	(9,643)
Chargeable gain	6,557

The net chargeable gain is therefore:
£(100 + 6,557 − 200) = £6,457

Working

	No. of shares	Cost
		£
10 August 2006 Acquisition	5,000	10,000
15 April 2009 Acquisition	2,000	5,000
	7,000	15,000
25 July 2014 Disposal	(4,500)	(9,643)
(£15,000 × 4,500/7,000 = £9,643)		
c/f	2,500	5,357

4   Her chargeable gain on sale is:

£	9,000

	£
Proceeds of sale	18,000
Less allowable cost (W)	(9,000)
Chargeable gain	**9,000**

Working

Share pool	No. of shares	Cost
		£
August 2004 Acquisition	2,000	10,000
May 2007 Rights issue 1 for 1 @ £2.50	2,000	5,000
(1/1 × 2,000 = 2,000 shares × £2.50 = £5,000)		
c/f	4,000	15,000
September 2010 Bonus 1 for 4	1,000	–
(1/4 × 4,000 = 1,000 shares)		
c/f	5,000	15,000
October 2014 Disposal	(3,000)	(9,000)
(£15,000 x 3,000/5,000 = £9,000)		
c/f	2,000	6,000

5

	✓
1,000 shares acquired on 9 October 2008, then with 1,000 shares acquired on 11 June 2010	
2,000 shares from the acquisitions in 2008 and 2010 in the FA 1985 pool	
2,000 shares from the acquisitions in 2008, 2010 and 2014 in the FA 1985 pool	
1,200 shares acquired on 12 July 2014, then with 800 shares in the FA 1985 pool	✓

6 (1)

	No of shares £	Cost £	Indexed cost £
10.8.05 Acquisition	3,000	9,000	9,000
Index to April 2007			
0.066 × £9,000			594
25.4.07 Acquisition	10,000	45,000	45,000
c/f	13,000	54,000	54,594
Index to September 2010			
0.097 × £54,594			5,296
			59,890
13.9.10 Disposal (× 1,000/13,000)	(1,000)	(4,154)	(4,607)
c/f	12,000	49,846	55,283
Index to November 2014			
0.149 × £55,283			8,237
			63,520
24.11.14 Disposal (× 8,500/12,000)	(8,500)	(35,308)	(44,993)
c/f	3,500	14,538	18,527

(2)

	£
Proceeds	47,200
Less cost	(35,308)
	11,892
Less indexation allowance £(44,993 − 35,308)	(9,685)
Chargeable gain	2,207

7   (1)

		No of shares	Cost £	Indexed cost £
5.03	Acquisition	10,000	45,000	45,000
10.05	Bonus 2:1	20,000		
		30,000		
6.09	Indexed rise			
	£45,000 × 0.176			7,920
	Rights 1:3 @ £4	10,000	40,000	40,000
		40,000	85,000	92,920
1.15	Indexed rise			
	£92,920 × 0.216			20,071
				112,991
	Disposal (20,000/40,000)	(20,000)	(42,500)	(56,496)
		20,000	42,500	56,495

(2)   The gain on sale is:

£   63,504

Workings:

	£
Proceeds	120,000
Less cost	(42,500)
	77,500
Less indexation allowance £(56,496 – 42,500)	(13,996)
Chargeable gain	**63,504**

CHAPTER 15   Reliefs for chargeable gains

1

	✓
Part of a business in which the individual has been a partner since August 2012	✓
A freehold factory which the individual uses in his business and has owned for 10 years	
Unquoted shares held by the individual in a personal trading company in which he is employed and which he has owned for the previous two years	✓
Quoted shares held by the individual in a personal trading company in which he is employed and which he has owned for the previous two years	✓

2   The CGT payable by Gwynneth is:

£	11,160

	£
Gains eligible for entrepreneurs' relief	50,000
Other gains	33,000
Chargeable gains	83,000
Less annual exempt amount	(11,000)
Taxable gains	72,000

CGT payable	
£50,000 × 10% (gains eligible for entrepreneurs' relief)	5,000
£22,000 × 28% (balance of other gains, no basic rate band remaining unused)	6,160
	11,160

3 (1)

	No of shares	Cost £
May 2004 Acquisition	10,000	50,000
August 2011 Acquisition	1,000	10,000
	11,000	60,000
July 2014 Disposal (2,200/11,000 × £60,000)	(2,200)	(12,000)
c/f	8,800	48,000

(2)

	£
Shares:	
Proceeds of sale	33,500
Less allowable cost (W)	(12,000)
Gain (eligible for entrepreneurs' relief)	21,500
Painting (not eligible for entrepreneurs' relief)	17,000
Less loss b/fwd	(1,300)
Less annual exempt amount	(11,000)
Taxable gain	26,200
CCT payable	
Shares: £21,500 @ 10%	2,150
Painting: £26,200 − £21,500 = £4,700 @ 28%	1,316
	3,466

4 (1) The gain on the sale of the factory in March 2015 is:

> £ | 55,000

	£
Sale proceeds	90,000
Less cost	(35,000)
Gain	55,000

(2) The gain that can be rolled over is:

> £ | 55,000

The amount invested was at least the same as the sale proceeds on disposal of the first factory.

(3) The base cost of the new factory acquired in April 2014 is:

> £ | 65,000

£(120,000 − 55,000)

5 (1) The gain on the sale of the office premises in May 2014 is:

> £ | 20,000

	£
Sale proceeds	100,000
Less cost	(80,000)
Gain	20,000

(2) The gain rolled over into the factory is:

> £ | 20,000

(3) The gain on the sale of the factory in September 2016 is:

> £ | 45,000

Factory

	£	£
Proceeds		375,000
Less cost	350,000	
Less rolled over gain	(20,000)	
Revised base cost		(330,000)
Gain		45,000

6   As a replacement factory is purchased in the period commencing one year before and ending three years after the sale of the first factory, rollover relief to defer the gain on the sale of the first factory can be claimed.

Rollover relief is restricted because the full proceeds of sale of the first factory are not reinvested. This means £20,000 £(670,000 – 650,000) of the gain on the first factory is immediately chargeable. The remaining gain of £100,000 is deducted from the base cost of the replacement factory. As a result any gain arising on the future sale of the replacement factory will be larger than it would have been had rollover relief not been claimed.

7   (1)   The gain on sale of the warehouse in August 2014 assuming that rollover relief is claimed is:

£	20,000

	£
Proceeds	120,000
Less cost	(75,000)
	45,000
Less indexation allowance 0.199 × £75,000	(14,925)
	30,075
Less rollover relief (balancing figure)	(10,075)
Chargeable gain: amount not reinvested	
£(120,000 – 100,000)	**20,000**

(2)   The base cost of the workshop is:

£	89,925

	£
Cost of workshop	100,000
Less rolled over gain	(10,075)
Base cost	89,925

8 (1) The gift relief on the gift made in December 2010 is:

£	320,000

	£
Deemed disposal proceeds	400,000
Less cost	(80,000)
Gain	320,000

(2) The gain on the sale in May 2014 is:

£	595,000

	£	£
Disposal proceeds		675,000
Less cost	400,000	
Gift relief	(320,000)	
		(80,000)
Gain		595,000

9

	✓
An antique painting	
Quoted shares in a trading company of which Deidre controls 1%	
Unquoted trading company shares	✓
A freehold factory that Deidre has always used in her printing business	✓

10 (1) If gift relief is not claimed, Julie's chargeable gain is:

£	35,000

	£
Deemed sale proceeds (MV)	85,000
Less cost	(50,000)
Gain	35,000

and Jack's chargeable gain is:

£	10,000

	£
Proceeds	95,000
Less cost (MV)	(85,000)
Gain	10,000

(2) If gift relief is claimed, Julie's chargeable gain is:

£	0

	£
Deemed sale proceeds	85,000
Less cost	(50,000)
	35,000
Less gift relief	(35,000)
Gain	0

and Jack's chargeable gain is:

£	45,000

	£	£
Proceeds		95,000
Less cost	85,000	
Less gift relief	(35,000)	
		(50,000)
Gain		45,000

TEST YOUR LEARNING – ANSWERS

CHAPTER 1   The tax framework

1

	✓
True	
False	✓

A company pays corporation tax on its total profits

2   Each tax year all of an individual's components of income are added together, then a personal allowance is deducted to arrive at **Taxable income**.

3

£	7,556

Non-savings income £	Savings income £	Dividend Income £	Total £
25,000			
	12,000		
		10,000	
25,000	12,000	10,000	47,000
(10,000)			(10,000)
15,000	12,000	10,000	37,000

Tax	£
Non-savings income	
£15,000 × 20%	3,000
Savings income	
£12,000 × 20%	2,400
Dividend income	
£4,865 × 10%	487
£5,135 × 32.5%	1,669
£10,000	**7,556**

CHAPTER 2 Computing trading income

1

	Allowable ✓
Legal fees incurred on the acquisition of a factory to be used for trade purposes	
Heating for factory	✓
Legal fees incurred on pursuing trade receivables	✓
Acquiring a machine to be used in the factory	

Legal fees on the acquisition of factory are capital expenditure and so not allowable. Heating is a revenue expense and so allowable. Legal fees incurred on pursuing trade receivables are allowable as they relate to a revenue source. Acquiring a machine is a capital expense and so not allowable (although capital allowances will be available for this expenditure).

2

£	700

The cost of staff entertaining is allowable. Gifts of food are never allowable. The entertaining of customers is never allowable.

3

	Allowable	Disallowable
Parking fines incurred by business owner		✓
Parking fines incurred by an employee whilst on the employer's business	✓	
Parking fines incurred by the director of a company whilst on company business		✓
Legal costs incurred in relation to acquiring a 10 year lease of property for the first time		✓
Legal costs incurred in relation to the renewal of a lease for 20 years	✓	
Gifts of calendars to customers, costing £4 each and displaying an advertisement for the company	✓	
Gifts of bottles of whisky to customers, costing £12 each		✓

4

	✓
£80 must be deducted from the accounts profit	
£80 must be added back to the accounts profit	
£96 must be deducted from the accounts profit	
£96 must be added back to the accounts profit	✓

The normal selling price of £80 + (20% × £80) = £96 must be added to the accounts profit.

5

£	700

Added back	Deducted
✓	✓
	✓

The movement on the general provision is disallowable (if an increase)/not taxable (if a decrease). This means that the decrease in the general provision of **£700** (£2,500 – £1,800) must be deducted from the accounts profit.

6

£	360

80% × £450 is disallowable for tax purposes.

CHAPTER 3   Capital allowances

1

£	2,000

A maximum of the original cost is deducted from the pool.

2

£	382,596

Workings:

Prorate AIA

Period to 5 April 2014 = £250,000 × 6/12 = £125,000

Period from 6 April 2014 = £500,000 × 6/12 = £250,000

The maximum AIA is the lower of the amount spent of £402,500 and the maximum for the period of £375,000 (£125,000 + £250,000).

Year ended 30 September 2014

	AIA	Main pool	Allowances
	£	£	£
B/f		22,500	
Addition qualifying for AIA			
Addition 1.5.14	402,500		
AIA (w)	(375,000)		375,000
Transfer balance to main pool		27,500	
Disposal			
Proceeds		(7,800)	
		42,200	
WDA @ 18%		(7,596)	7,596
C/f		34,604	
Allowances			**382,596**

3

£	6,620

6 months ended 31 December 2014

	FYA @ 100% £	Main pool £	Allowances £
Addition (no AIA)		18,000	
WDA @ 18% × 6/12		(1,620)	1,620
		16,380	
Addition	5,000		
FYA @ 100%	(5,000)		5,000
C/f		16,380	
			6,620

Note. The AIA and WDAs are time apportioned in a short period. FYAs are not. AIAs and FYAs are not available on a car with CO_2 emissions of 115g/km.

4

	✓
True	
False	✓

There is no AIA or WDA in the final period so a **balancing allowance** arises as follows:

	£
B/f	12,500
Addition	20,000
Proceeds	(18,300)
	14,200
Balancing allowance	**(14,200)**

5

£	1,440

Year ended 30 April 2015

	Private use asset @ 60% £	Allowances £
Addition	30,000	
WDA @ 8%	(2,400) × 60%	**1,440**
C/f	27,600	

CHAPTER 4 Taxing unincorporated businesses

1

Tax year	Basis period
2014/15	1 May 2014 – 5 April 2015
2015/16	Year ended 31 December 2015
2016/17	Year ended 31 December 2016
Overlap profits	1 January 2015 – 5 April 2015

2

	✓
True	✓
False	

When the trade ceases overlap profits are deducted from the final tax year's taxable profits.

3

Tax year	Basis period	Taxable profits £
2012/13	1 June 2011 to 31 May 2012	18,000
2013/14	1 June 2012 to 31 May 2013	32,000
2014/15	1 June 2013 – 31 December 2014	30,000

In 2014/15, taxable profits are (£25,000 + £15,000 – £10,000) = £30,000

4

Tax year	Basis period	Taxable profits £
2013/14	1 February 2014 – 5 April 2014	34,000 x 2/17 = 4,000
2014/15	6 April 2014 – 5 April 2015	34,000 x 12/17 = 24,000
2015/16	12 months ended 30 June 2015	34,000 x 12/17 = 24,000

His overlap profits are:

£	18,000

(1 July 2014 to 5 April 2015)

9/17 × £34,000

5 (1) Her taxable profits for 2013/14 are:

£ | 40,000

(1 December 2013 – 5 April 2014)   4/7 × £70,000

(2) Her taxable profits for 2014/15 are:

£ | 95,000

(1 December 2013 – 30 November 2014) £70,000 + 5/12 × £60,000

(3) Her taxable profits for 2015/16 are:

£ | 60,000

(1 July 2014 to 30 June 2015)

(4) Her overlap profits are:

£ | 65,000

	£
1 December 2013 – 5 April 2014	40,000
1 July 2014 – 30 November 2014	25,000
	65,000

CHAPTER 5   Partnerships

1

	✓
The calendar year	
The tax year	
The period of account concerned	✓
The period agreed by the partners	

2

Dave's taxable profits for 2014/15 are:

£	9,450

and Joe's taxable profits for 2014/15 are:

£	8,550

Working:

	Total £	Dave £	Joe £
1.1.14 – 30.9.14 (9/12)	13,500	6,750	6,750
1.10.14– 31.12.14 (3/12)	4,500	2,700	1,800
	18,000	**9,450**	**8,550**

3

	Total £	Holly £	Jasmine £
Salary	85,000	5,000	80,000
Division of profits 1:1	115,000	57,500	57,500
	200,000	62,500	137,500

4

	✓
£60,000	
£15,000	
£45,000	
£20,000	✓

2014/15 (year ended 31 March 2015)

Taxable profits on Steve for 2014/15 are £20,000 (1/4 × £80,000).

5 The profits assessable on Sase in 2014/15 are:

£	14,000

The opening year rules apply to Sase. *(1 September 2014 – 5 April 2015)*
7/12 × £24,000

The profits assessable on Sase in 2015/16 are:

£	24,000

(year ended 31 August 2015)

The overlap profits arising for Sase are:

£	14,000

Workings: Year ended 31 August 2015

	Total £	Abdul £	Ghita £	Sase £
Profits (2:2:1)	120,000	48,000	48,000	24,000

6 (1)

	Total £	William £	Ann £	John £
Y/e 31.10.13	21,000	7,000	7,000	7,000
Y/e 31.10.14	33,000	11,000	11,000	11,000
Y/e 31.10.15				
1.11.14 – 31.12.14 (2/12)	6,000	2,000	2,000	2,000
1.1.15 – 31.10.15 (10/12)	30,000	0	15,000	15,000
	36,000	2,000	17,000	17,000

(2)

	William £	Ann £	John £
2013/14 (y/e 31 October 2013)	7,000	7,000	7,000
2014/15 (y/e 31 October 2014)	8,000	11,000	11,000
2015/16 (y/e 31 October 2015)	0	17,000	17,000

Ann and John will be taxed on the current year basis of assessment throughout. The cessation rules apply to William in 2014/15, the year he left the business:

1 November 2013 – 31 December 2014 (£11,000 + £2,000 – £5,000) = £8,000

CHAPTER 6   Computing taxable total profits

1

Type of income	True	False
A company with a nine month period of account will calculate capital allowances for nine months and deduct them from adjusted trading profits.	✓	
A company with an eighteen month period of account will calculate capital allowances for eighteen months and deduct them from adjusted trading profits, and then prorate the answer between the appropriate accounting periods.		✓
A company with an eighteen month period of account will calculate capital allowances for the first twelve months then capital allowances for the remaining six months and deduct them from the relevant prorated trading profits allocated to each accounting period.	✓	
Dividends are not included in the taxable total profits. They are taxed separately.		✓

Capital allowances are calculated separately for each accounting period and then deducted from the prorated adjusted profits.

Dividends are not taxable for the company (for the purpose of the Business Tax assessment).

2

	✓
Added to trading income	
Added to net non-trading interest	
Deducted from trading income	✓
Deducted from net non-trading interest	

The loan is for trading purposes and is interest PAID, not received, so it is included as an expense.

3

£	385

Companies make donations gross.

4

	✓
1 June 2013 – 31 March 2014 and 1 April 2014 – 31 August 2014	
1 June 2013 – 31 May 2014 and 1 June 2014– 31 August 2014	✓
1 June 2013 – 31 December 2013 and 1 January 2014 – 31 August 2014	
1 June 2013 – 31 August 2013 and 1 September 2013 – 31 August 2014	

The first accounting period is always 12 months in length in a long accounting period.

5

	Year ended 31.12.14 £	4 months ended 30.4.15 £
Trading profits (12/16 : 4/16)	240,000	80,000
Interest (accrued for each period)	1,200	400
Chargeable gain (allocate to period made)	0	20,000
Qualifying charitable donation (allocate to period paid)	(15,000)	0
Taxable total profits	226,200	100,400

CHAPTER 7 Computing corporation tax payable

1

£	52,312

	£
Taxable total profits	255,000
Dividend	–
Augmented profits	255,000

Lower limit £300,000 × 6/12 = £150,000

Upper limit £1,500,000 × 6/12 = £750,000

As this is a six month period, the limits are multiplied by 6/12.

Marginal relief applies:

FY14

	£
£255,000 × 21%	53,550
Less 1/400 £(750,000 – 255,000)	(1,238)
	52,312

2

£	10,000

Augmented profits = £55,000

Lower limit £300,000 × 9/12 = £225,000

Small profits rate applies:

FY14

£50,000 × 20% = **£10,000**

3

£	101,562

1) Taxable total profits/ augmented profits are £490,000.

   This means marginal relief applies.

2) With a year ended 31 December 2014, 3 months fall into FY13 and 9 months fall into FY14.

3) Tax on taxable total profits (FY 2013)

   £490,000 × 23% × 3/12 =£28,175

   Less 3/400 £(1,500,000 – 490,000) × 3/12 =£(1,894)

Tax on taxable total profits (FY 2014)

£490,000 × 21% × 9/12 = £77,175

Less 1/400 £(1,500,000 – 490,000) × 9/12 = £(1,894)

Total CT liability = £28,175 less £(1,894) + £77,175 less £(1,894)

= **£101,562**

4

£	36,844

Taxable total profits = £180,000

Lower limit £300,000/2 × 9/12 = £112,500

Upper limit £1,500,000/2 × 9/12 = £562,500

There are two associated companies, so the limits are divided by 2. The limits are also multiplied by 9/12 as this is a short accounting period.

Marginal relief applies:

	£
FY14	
£180,000 × 21%	37,800
Less 1/400 £(562,500 – 180,000)	(956)
	36,844

5

	✓
True	✓
False	

Financial Year 2014 (FY14) begins on 1 April 2014 and ends on 31 March 2015.

CHAPTER 8   Losses

1

	✓
2014/15 only	
2015/16 and/or 2014/15	
2013/14 only	
2014/15 and/or 2013/14	✓

2

	✓
True	
False	✓

Trading losses can be carried forward indefinitely.

3

	✓
Against non-savings income	
Against total income	
Against trading income arising in the same trade	✓
Against trading income arising in all trades carried on by the taxpayer	

4   The loss is a loss of 2014/15.

It can be:

(a)   Deducted from total income of £9,000 in 2014/15 and/or from total income of £19,000 in 2013/14.

(b)   Carried forward to be deducted from taxable trading profits of £25,000 in 2015/16 and then in later years.

5

(1) The amount of trading loss remaining to be carried forward at 1 November 2014 assuming that all possible loss relief claims against total profits are made is:

£	(85,000)

(£320,000 – £60,000 – £175,000)

	Year ended 31 October	
	2013	2014
	£	£
Trading profit	170,000	0
Interest	5,000	60,000
Capital gain £(12,000 – 20,000)	0	0
Total profits	175,000	60,000
Less current period loss relief	0	(60,000)
Less carry back loss relief	(175,000)	0
Less Qualifying charitable donation	0	0
	0	0
	5,000	5,000
Unrelieved qualifying charitable donations		

(2) The amount of capital loss remaining to be carried forward at 1 November 2014 is:

£	(8,000)

(£20,000 – £12,000)

6

	✓
£Nil	
£2,000	✓
£4,000	
£3,000	

	Year ended 31.3.13 £	Six months 30.9.13 £	Year ended 30.9.14 £
Trading profit	4,000	6,000	0
Less current period loss relief	0	0	0
carry back loss relief	(2,000)	(6,000)	0
qualifying charitable donation	(1,000)	–	–
Taxable total profits	1,000	–	–

The maximum relief for year ended 31.3.13 is £4,000 × 6/12

CHAPTER 9   National Insurance

1   Acker

£	00	.	00

No Class 2 NICs as earnings below small earnings exception

No Class 4 NICs due as profits below annual lower profits limit of £7,956

2   Bailey

£	3,357	.	51

		£
Class 2 NICs	52 × £2.75	143.00
Class 4 NICs	(£41,865 – £7,956) × 9%	3,051.81
	(£50,000 – £41,865) × 2%	162.70
Total NICs		**3,357.51**

3   Cartwright

£	403	.	46

Class 2 NICs 52 × £2.75 = £143.00

Class 4 NICs (£10,850 – £7,956) × 9% = £260.46

Total NICs = **£403.46**

CHAPTER 10   Self assessment for individuals

1   The due filing date for an income tax return for 2014/15 assuming the taxpayer will submit the return online is

31/01/16

2

The 2014/15 payments on account will be calculated as

50%

of the income tax payable and Class 4 NICs for

2013/14

and will be due on

31 January 2015

and

31 July 2015

3   £100 penalty for failure to deliver return on time.

Possible £10 per day penalty from 1 May 2016 until date of filing.

5% penalty on tax paid late. Interest on tax paid late.

4

	✓
31 January 2017	
31 March 2017	
6 April 2017	
28 January 2017	✓

A year after the actual filing date because Susie filed the return before the due filing date (31 January 2016).

5

Jamie's 2014/15 payments on account will each be

| £6,000 |

and will be due on (insert date as XX/XX/XX)

| 31/01/15 |

and

| 31/07/15 |

Jamie's balancing payment will be

| £4,000 |

and will be due on (insert date as XX/XX/XX)

| 31/01/16 |

6

| £ | 0 |

No penalties for late payment are due on late payments on account.

7

(1) By what date must a taxpayer generally submit a tax return for 2014/15 if it is filed as a paper return?

	✓
30 September 2015	
31 October 2015	✓
31 December 2015	
31 January 2016	

Paper returns must usually be submitted by 31 October following the end of the tax year.

(2) On which dates are payment on accounts due for 2014/15?

	✓
31 January 2016 and 31 July 2016	
31 January 2015 and 31 July 2015	✓
31 October 2015 and 31 January 2016	
31 July 2015 and 31 January 2016	

Payments on account are due on 31 January in the tax year and 31 July following the end of the tax year.

8

	✓
£5,100	
£3,400	
£1,020	✓
£2,380	

30% × PLR = **£1,020**

PLR = £17,000 × 20% = £3,400

CHAPTER 11 Self assessment for companies

1

1 June 2016

(12 months after the actual filing date)

2

£	100

(The return is less than 3 months late)

3

	✓
14 July 2014	
1 October 2015	✓
31 December 2015	
1 January 2016	

Girton Ltd is a small company, so all CT is due nine months and one day after the end of the accounting period.

4

	✓
14 April 2015	
14 April 2016	
14 July 2015	✓
1 October 2016	

Eaton Ltd is a large company and is required to pay corporation tax by instalments. The first instalment is due in the seventh month of the accounting period.

5

£	60,000

1/4 × £240,000

CHAPTER 12   Chargeable gains – the basics

1

	Chargeable ✓	Exempt ✓
A gift of an antique necklace	✓	
The sale of a building	✓	

2   Her chargeable gain on sale is:

£	235,000

	£
Proceeds	560,000
Less cost	(325,000)
Chargeable gain	235,000

3   The amount liable to CGT in 2014/15 is:

£	144,700

The losses carried forward are:

£	0

	£
Gains	171,000
Less current year losses	(5,300)
	165,700
Less losses b/f	(10,000)
	155,700
Less annual exempt amount	(11,000)
Taxable gains	144,700

4   Martha's CGT liability for 2014/15 is:

£	3,612

	£
Chargeable gains	23,900
Less annual exempt amount	(11,000)
Taxable gains	12,900
CGT on £12,900 @ 28%	3,612

5   The payment date for capital gains tax for 2014/15 is (insert date as XX/XX/XX):

> 31/01/16

6   Indexation allowance runs from **the date the expenditure was incurred** to **the date of disposal**.

7

	£
Proceeds of sale	200,000
Less cost	(80,000)
Less enhancement expenditure	(10,000)
	110,000
Less indexation allowance on cost £80,000 × 0.341	(27,280)
Less indexation allowance on enhancement £10,000 × 0.205	(2,050)
Chargeable gain	80,670

CHAPTER 13   Further aspects of chargeable gains

1   The chargeable gain/allowable loss arising is:

	✓
£16,663	✓
£17,500	
£19,663	
£18,337	

	£
Proceeds	38,000
Less costs of disposal	(3,000)
	35,000
Less £41,500 × $\frac{38,000}{38,000 + 48,000}$	(18,337)
Chargeable gain	16,663

2   The gain arising if he sells it for:

(a)   £5,800 after deducting selling expenses of £180 is:

£	Nil

There is no gain as the chattel is sold for gross proceeds of less than £6,000.

(b)   £8,200 after deducting selling expenses of £220 is:

£	4,033

	£
Gross proceeds	8,420
Less selling expenses	(220)
Net proceeds	8,200
Less cost	(3,500)
	4,700

Gain cannot exceed 5/3 (8,420 – 6,000) = £4,033
Therefore, gain is £4,033

3   The gain arising is:

£	Nil

A racehorse is an exempt asset as it is a wasting chattel, so no chargeable gain or allowable loss arises.

4   The loss arising is:

£	(1,000)

	£
Deemed proceeds	6,000
Less cost	(7,000)
Allowable loss	(1,000)

5

(1)   The cost of the part of the land sold is:

£	20,000

$$\frac{80,000}{80,000 + 120,000} \times £50,000 = \underline{\mathbf{£20,000}}$$

(2)   The chargeable gain arising on the disposal is:

£	56,040

	£
Proceeds of sale	80,000
Less cost (W)	(20,000)
	60,000
Less indexation allowance £20,000 × 0.198	(3,960)
Chargeable gain	**56,040**

6 The gain arising is:

£	3,333

	£
Proceeds of sale	8,000
Less cost	(3,500)
	4,500
Less indexation allowance £3,500 × 0.065	(228)
Chargeable gain	4,272
Gain cannot exceed £(8,000 – 6,000) × 5/3	**3,333**

7

	£
Deemed proceeds of sale	6,000
Less cost	(8,700)
Allowable loss	**(2,700)**

	✓
£(5,923)	
£(4,400)	
£(2,700)	✓
£(4,223)	

8

	✓
True	
False	✓

A loss on a disposal to a connected person can be set only against gains arising on disposals to the same connected person.

9 No gain or loss arises on a disposal to a spouse/civil partner.

	✓
True	✓
False	

10

	Actual proceeds used	Deemed proceeds (market value) used	No gain or loss basis
Paul sells an asset to his civil partner Joe for £3,600			✓
Grandmother gives an asset to her grandchild worth £1,000		✓	
Sarah sells an asset to best friend Cathy for £12,000 worth £20,000		✓	

CHAPTER 14   Share disposals

1   Her chargeable gain is:

	✓
£15,750	
£11,500	
£17,000	
£14,250	✓

	No. of shares	Cost
	£	£
August 1993 Acquisition	10,000	5,000
April 2008 Acquisition	10,000	16,000
	20,000	21,000
November 2014 Disposal	(15,000)	(15,750)
(£21,000 × 15,000/20,000 = £15,750)		
c/f	5,000	5,250

	£
Proceeds of sale	30,000
Less allowable cost	(15,750)
Chargeable gain	**14,250**

2

	✓
True	
False	✓

In a rights issue, shares are paid for and this amount is added to the original cost. In a bonus issue, shares are not paid for and so there is no adjustment to the original cost.

3   His chargeable gain is:

£	3,750

No. of shares		*Cost*
		£
May 2002 Acquisition	2,000	12,000
December 2003 1 for 2 rights issue @ £7.50	1,000	7,500
(1/2 × 2,000 = 1,000 shares × £7.50 = £7,500)		
	3,000	19,500
March 2015 Disposal	(2,500)	(16,250)
(£19,500 × 2,500/3,000)		
c/f	500	3,250

	£
Proceeds of sale	20,000
Less allowable costs	(16,250)
Chargeable gain	**3,750**

4   Her chargeable gain is:

£	7,000

	No. of shares	*Cost*
		£
June 2010 Acquisition	6,000	15,000
August 2011 1 for 3 bonus issue	2,000	nil
(1/3 × 6,000 = 2,000 shares)		
	8,000	15,000
December 2014 Disposal (ie all the shares)	(8,000)	(15,000)
c/f	nil	nil

	£
Proceeds of sale	22,000
Less allowable costs	(15,000)
Chargeable gain	**7,000**

5   The matching rules for shares disposed of by a company shareholder are:

(a)   Shares acquired on the same day
(b)   Shares acquired in the previous nine days (FIFO)
(c)   Shares from the FA 1985 pool

6 (1)

		No of shares	Cost £	Indexed cost £
5.03	Acquisition	10,000	90,000	90,000
6.09	Indexed rise			
	£90,000 × 0.176			15,840
	Rights 1:4 @ £12	2,500	30,000	30,000
		12,500	120,000	135,840
1.15	Indexed rise			
	£135,840 × 0.216			29,341
				165,181
	Disposal (× 10,000/12,500)	(10,000)	(96,000)	(132,145)
		2,500	24,000	33,036

(2)

	£
Proceeds	150,000
Less cost	(96,000)
	54,000
Less indexation allowance £(132,145 – 96,000)	(36,145)
Chargeable gain	17,855

CHAPTER 15   Reliefs for chargeable gains

1   Ian's CGT liability for 2014/15 is:

£	1,108,920

	£
Gains	10,400,000
Less annual exempt amount	(11,000)
Chargeable gain	10,389,000
CGT:	
10,000,000 @ 10%	1,000,000
389,000 @ 28%	108,920
	1,108,920

2   Jemma's CGT on the disposal, assuming she has already used the annual exempt amount for 2014/15, is:

£	7,000

	£
Proceeds of sale	80,000
Less allowable cost	(10,000)
Taxable gain (no annual exempt amount available)	70,000
CGT @ 10%	**7,000**

3

	✓
Office block	
Freehold factory	✓
Fork lift truck	
Freehold warehouse	

The office block and the freehold warehouse were acquired outside the qualifying reinvestment period commencing one year before and ending three years after the disposal.

The fork lift truck is not fixed plant and machinery.

4

	✓
£120,000	
£200,000	
£400,000	✓
£420,000	

Land

	£
Sales proceeds	400,000
Less cost	(100,000)
Gain	300,000

£20,000 of the proceeds are not reinvested, so £20,000 of the gain remains chargeable, £280,000 is rolled over.

Replacement land

	£	£
Sale proceeds		500,000
Less cost	380,000	
Rolled over gain	(280,000)	
Revised base cost		(100,000)
Chargeable gain		400,000

5

	✓
True	✓
False	

6

If relief for replacement of business assets is to be claimed, reinvestment of the proceeds must take place in a period beginning

12	months before and ending	36

months after the date of disposal.

7 The chargeable gain after rollover relief is:

£	25,000

The gain on the sale of first warehouse is:

	£
Proceeds	400,000
Less cost	(220,000)
	180,000
Less indexation allowance	(40,000)
	140,000
Less rollover relief (balancing figure)	(115,000)
Chargeable gain: amount not reinvested £(400,000 – 375,000)	**25,000**

8

	✓
True	
False	✓

Jewellery is not a qualifying asset for gift relief purposes.

9 If gift relief is claimed, the gain on the gift by Tommy is:

£	0

	£
Market value	200,000
Less cost	(50,000)
Gain	150,000
Less gift relief	(150,000)
Gain left in charge	**0**

and the gain on the sale by Sinbad is:

£	300,000

	£
Sale proceeds	350,000
Less cost (£200,000 – £150,000)	(50,000)
Gain	**300,000**

INDEX

INDEX

Notes

REVIEW FORM

How have you used this Text?
(Tick one box only)

☐ Home study

☐ On a course_____

☐ Other _____

Why did you decide to purchase this Text? *(Tick one box only)*

☐ Have used BPP Texts in the past

☐ Recommendation by friend/colleague

☐ Recommendation by a college lecturer

☐ Saw advertising

☐ Other _____

During the past six months do you recall seeing/receiving either of the following?
(Tick as many boxes as are relevant)

☐ Our advertisement in Accounting Technician

☐ Our Publishing Catalogue

Which (if any) aspects of our advertising do you think are useful?
(Tick as many boxes as are relevant)

☐ Prices and publication dates of new editions

☐ Information on Text content

☐ Details of our free online offering

☐ None of the above

Your ratings, comments and suggestions would be appreciated on the following areas of this Text.

	Very useful	Useful	Not useful
Introductory section	☐	☐	☐
Quality of explanations	☐	☐	☐
How it works	☐	☐	☐
Chapter tasks	☐	☐	☐
Chapter Overviews	☐	☐	☐
Test your learning	☐	☐	☐
Index	☐	☐	☐

	Excellent	Good	Adequate	Poor
Overall opinion of this Text	☐	☐	☐	☐

Do you intend to continue using BPP Products? ☐ Yes ☐ No

Please note any further comments and suggestions/errors on the reverse of this page. The publishing manager of this edition can be emailed at: ianblackmore@bpp.com

Please return to: Ian Blackmore, AAT Range Manager, BPP Learning Media Ltd, FREEPOST, London, W12 8AA.

REVIEW FORM (continued)

TELL US WHAT YOU THINK

Please note any further comments and suggestions/errors below.